Paul Nelson's book is a timely reminder to Christians all over the world that the faith was founded by God Himself, that because Our Lord is the Truth, there can be no contradiction in Him or His teachings, and because of this, we are all called to be one in Christ.

Since Christianity has been divided along theological, philosophical, and understandings of hierarchy and authority, it is imperative that those divisions are healed by clear demarcations of Truth.

During this time of great confusion and uncertainty, Nelson draws on his own personal experience to provide a clear and succinct path for those whose faith is wavering and to draw in those who are away from the Church.

Michael Hichborn, President
Lepanto Institute

CHRISTIANS MUST REUNITE
Now Is the Time

Paul A. Nelson

LEONINE PUBLISHERS
PHOENIX, ARIZONA

Cover image: "Sermon on the Mount" painting, by Carl Bloch, licensed under CC BY-SA 3.0 (https://commons.wikimedia.org/wiki/File:Bloch-SermonOnTheMount.jpg).

Scripture citations are from *The Ignatius Catholic Study Bible*, Revised Standard Version, copyright © 2010 by Ignatius Press, San Francisco.

Published by Leonine Publishers LLC
Phoenix, Arizona
USA

ISBN-13: 978-1-942190-56-1

Library of Congress Control Number: 2019911950

10 9 8 7 6 5 4 3 2 1

Visit us online at www.leoninepublishers.com
For more information: info@leoninepublishers.com

Dedicated to

Our Lord Jesus Christ;
my wife, Nancy;
and my children, Heather, Erin, and Pete.
I love them all dearly.

Contents

Foreword

I met Paul Nelson, a convert to Catholicism, in 2012 when he attended a Cursillo (meaning a short course in Christianity) weekend where I was one of the team leaders. Over the years, we have grown to be close friends and I often look to Paul for spiritual direction in my own life. As a Marian Catechist, Paul has spent countless hours learning about his Catholic faith and how to apply Church teaching daily. He challenges all to fully live out their faith.

Now is the time! Paul engages and challenges readers to live the fullness of Truth in their lives by fully understanding the teachings of Christ Himself and how these truths are revealed through the Magisterium of the Church. He shares the struggles of his own spiritual journey and how the Holy Spirit has formed his heart over the years. He invites all Christians to study the Bible with fervor and see the beauty of all Catholic doctrine.

Paul shares the depth and history of Catholic tradition while at the same time delving into the current problems of today that are eroding Christianity. He offers a scriptural basis for Church teaching and how we should apply these teachings in our own life to overcome difficulties. The author's passion and love for the Lord and His Church are on full display in this book.

Paul covers important core teachings of the Catholic Church and provides readers with many thought-provoking questions along the way. He invites all of us to reunite and become one mighty presence on earth for Jesus Christ. In a world of moral relativism that creates obstacles to holiness, we need authentic teaching on social justice and on living a morally authentic life. We are all called to find our identity in Jesus and not in the culture of self-indulgence. This book offers readers an opportunity to examine their own lives and find the fullness of who they were created to be—a child of God.

~ Rev. Mr. David A. Reaves
July 23, 2019

Main Purpose of This Book

We are at a crucial time in the history of the world when we must very carefully assess the way we live and examine our religious beliefs very closely. The evil that is taking place all around us is increasing at a frenetic pace, and much of it is being commonly accepted and even included in our laws. The fact that Christianity is being pushed to the background and virtually ignored should be a wake-up call to every human being of faith.

Were you aware that during the twentieth century more people died for the faith than in all previous centuries combined? The Christian Church has been infiltrated by heretics and false teachers like never before. The number of people actually inside the Church seeking to destroy it is staggering.

If there were ever a time for all Christians to reunite and become one mighty presence on earth for Jesus Christ, THIS is the time! Now, I realize that to make that happen a lot of hurdles will need to be gotten over, and a willingness to keep an open mind is absolutely necessary.

This book is written by a Catholic, yes, but my effort is just as much for the millions of Protestants who worship and love Christ. To the Catholics reading this, I say study and learn your faith more deeply. It will be very fruitful and will improve your life in every possible way. Believe me, you don't know what you don't know! Think about that.

I ask any Protestants reading this to give me a chance to make my case for reunification. I consider you all brothers and sisters in Christ, make no mistake about that. Please read this book, check my resources and assertions, pray for guidance, and then make your decision.

Introduction

This work is my personal attempt to lay out as clearly as I can the truths within the Church's teachings. Years ago, I was an ignorant Catholic, and I fell prey to false teaching and secular beliefs, and I was caught up in the trappings of this world, completely ignoring the world to come. I knew very little then of Christ and His Church and was satisfied with the status quo. It is crucial that we as Catholic Christians study the Church; our very salvation depends on knowing and adhering to Christ's teachings. What could be more important?

The Catholic Church is under attack more now than at any other time in its history. Yes, it has been threatened from the very beginning, but this problem is accelerating at an alarming pace in recent decades. I make an appeal to all Catholics to decide to get to know your Church more intimately. And I sincerely implore all Protestants to study the history of the Christian Church with an open mind. I am confident that you'll find that the Reformation was not only unnecessary, it was heretical. I respectfully challenge you all to study and pray for guidance. If you reject Catholicism after doing so, I will be very surprised. I believe you will discover that Martin Luther, John Calvin, and the other so-called "reformers" were wrong to do what they did. If you desire the truth and pursue it prayerfully, I believe you'll find the complete truth within the Catholic Church.

CHAPTER 1

False Teaching

The Bible warns us over and over of future false teaching and heresies. Saint Paul told his protégé Timothy:

> For the time is coming when people will not endure sounding teaching, but having itching ears they will accumulate for themselves teachers to suit their own likings, and will turn away from listening to the truth and wander into myths (Timothy 4:3-4).

There have been heresies from the very beginning, such as Gnosticism in the first and second centuries, Montanism in the mid-second century, Sabellianism in the third century, Arianism in the fourth century, and many more over the succeeding centuries. If one wishes to learn about those particular heresies, there is a lot of material available. The Protestant heresy began in the very early sixteenth century, and it has been the most successful one, because it continues today. Yes, Protestantism is a heresy. Stay with me and I'll make my case.

At the time of Luther's revolt against the Church, some bishops were abusing their positions, and even

3

the pope was distorting the faith in some cases. Sinful acts by many in the Church's hierarchy were rampant. Ultimately, though, Luther's grave mistake was breaking with the Church and basically starting his own version of it. It is written by some that his initial intention was not to separate from the Church, but that ended up being the unfortunate result.

Remember, John 14:26 states generally that the Father will send the Holy Spirit to teach the Apostles and their successors all things. In John 16:12-13, Jesus says, "I have yet many things to say to you, but you cannot bear them now. When the Spirit of truth comes, he will guide you into all the truth." In Matthew 28:18-20, Jesus said to the Apostles after His resurrection:

> All authority in heaven and on earth has been given to me. Go therefore and make disciples of all nations, baptizing them in the name of the Father and of the Son and of the Holy Spirit, teaching them to observe all that I have commanded you; and behold, I am with you always, to the close of the age.

One can clearly see from these quotes that it is absolutely biblical to conclude that the Father would send the Holy Spirit to guide the Church in the truth until the end of time. Jesus obviously passed on His authority to baptize and teach to the Apostles and their successors, telling them the Holy Spirit would guide them. It would be foolish indeed and very shortsighted to believe that the Apostles didn't pass on the same authority given them to their successors. That process continues to this day in the ordination of new priests. Let's face it, Jesus did not say the Holy Spirit would guide the Church until 1517, when Martin Luther became disillusioned with certain practices going on within the Church and decided to just start another version. When Jesus said "to the close of the age," He meant just that.

My intent here is not to bash our Protestant brothers and sisters. Most of them have been born into a Protestant family and that's all they have known. I know most of them love Jesus and have strong faith. They may not be aware of what is missing in their version of Christianity. Many Protestant denominations (and there are tens of thousands) are vehemently anti-Catholic due to the myths and misinformation they have been fed. Others actually believe Catholics are Christians, too. An important point to re-emphasize is that there are over 30,000 different Protestant denominations, and their Bible teachings and interpretations of scripture vary widely. Do you think that's what Christ envisioned when He said the Holy Spirit would guide the Church in all truth? I suggest the answer to that is no. Make no mistake, Martin Luther and the others who conspired with him became heretics. They and their successors have desecrated and distorted Christ's Church. And their teachings have evolved over the centuries into something even they wouldn't recognize.

I will make my case that Catholicism is the only way to go if you want the fullness of the Christian Church passed on to us. In John 17, Jesus prayed to the Father fervently, asking several times for unity in the Church. The Reformation never should have happened.

We as Christians need to honor Christ's desire that we "may become perfectly one" (John 17:23).

Unfortunately, many Catholics do not read the Bible very much, but in my observation this seems to be changing, thankfully. Protestants read the Bible often, which is great. The problem is that they misinterpret many very important verses. In fact, the Lutheran church may interpret something far differently than a Baptist church does. The reason for this situation is that there is no ultimate authority regarding interpreting scripture in Protestantism. Pastors from the various denominations often interpret Bible passages differently, and even individuals are encouraged to make their own interpretations, based on "how the Spirit moves you." How can the truth be interpreted in different ways? In fact, it cannot be. Remember, Jesus gave authority to the Apostles and their successors to teach the truth as they themselves learned it. The Holy Spirit has been, and still is, guiding the Catholic Church in all truth, and it will do so until the end of time.

In the following chapters, I will discuss many of the issues that divide Christians. My hope and desire is to help strengthen the faith and enhance the knowledge of Catholics about their Church. My goal is also to convince Protestants to come home to the fullness of the Christian Church, which is the Catholic Church. Now, more than ever, we all need to unify, as Jesus Christ desired way back during His earnest prayer in John 17. The situation for Christians in the world is dire, and the Lord is counting on us.

CHAPTER 2

My Story

B efore getting into my sincere advocacy and defense of the Catholic Church, I feel it is important to explain my zeal with a personal story. Without a doubt, I have been called to a deeper relationship with God and given the task that I am undertaking here.

I come from a family of five children. Mom was a cradle Catholic; Dad was a Protestant. They couldn't agree on religion, and the unfortunate result was that we never attended any church as a family. At the age of sixteen, I began dating my wonderful Nancy. She and her mother were devout Catholics, and they invited me to attend Mass with them. Some months later, I approached my parents and asked if I could take instructions to become a Catholic. Mom was elated, and Dad reluctantly gave his permission. My three older siblings had already become Catholic. My younger brother, Bill, was permitted to go to instructions with me, so that made it unanimous.

From his many remarks, I knew Dad wasn't happy about all of his kids choosing Catholicism, but he just surrendered at that point. Interestingly though, when my brother and I were baptized, received our First Holy

Communion, and were confirmed, Dad was there in the church, and he even wore a tie! When he smiled at me, I have to tell you that I felt some relief and maybe even a little affirmation.

Back then, the extent of our instruction in the faith consisted of a meeting/class once a week for three months. Many of the essential points that the priest made went right over our heads. As a result, my little brother and I joined the ranks of the many other poorly catechized Catholics. Even the kids who attended Catholic schools didn't understand the Church well, and most of them certainly didn't read the Bible. I don't remember having one in our house.

Nancy and I married in 1974, when I was twenty-one and she was nineteen. She was always the one dragging me to church, even after we started having children. I just didn't think it was important to attend every Sunday. After all, I was a good person, right?

In about 1982, Nancy and I were invited to attend a weekend retreat—they called it a "renewal"—at our parish. Men and women had separate weekends. Nancy's came first. Frankly, I signed up reluctantly because a friend asked me to. But what I witnessed at the closing of Nancy's retreat gave me a new outlook. The participants processed into the church carrying candles. There was a very distinct holiness in the faces of those women. When I looked into the eyes of my wife, I knew that I wanted and needed whatever it was that she experienced. My experience at the men's renewal definitely took my faith to a higher level and inspired me to learn more. Also, we made dear friends during our retreat weekends that endure to this day, even though we moved away from that area years ago.

In the years to follow, I did enjoy Mass more, and I actually read the Bible once in a while. There came a time when my focus turned inward. I studied self-improvement and motivation. I bought all the books and tapes, and my goal was to make a lot of money and be "successful." I studied real estate investing, stock investing, and any other vehicle that would take me where I thought I needed to be. I used visualization techniques, seeing myself with a mansion, expensive cars, and the ability to travel the world. I wanted the respect of other human beings. I truly believed that "whatever you can conceive, you can achieve." Right? Not really.

Although I attended Mass with my family on Sunday, I was preoccupied with achieving success in the secular world. I did fairly well in several investment endeavors and in my profession as a court reporter, but there was something missing that I couldn't put my finger on. Probably because of my obsession with motivation and the like, I started to get bored in church. The priest spoke in a monotone, and I felt I needed upbeat preaching—you know, something motivational.

At the time, Nancy was attending a program with a friend at a local Baptist church. It was open to anyone interested in attending. She met the pastor there and told me he was charismatic and nice. He extended an invitation to her and me to attend services at his church just to check it out. I think Nancy was surprised when I said maybe we should give his church a try; after all, it's still a Christian church, right?

We attended that Baptist church the next Sunday, forsaking the Holy Mass. Well, I want to tell you that it was amazing! Everyone stood and sang uplifting songs; the words were even up on a big screen for all to follow. The pastor was a big man, dressed impeccably. He moved quickly around the stage and spoke loudly and with conviction. He was apparently in the middle of a series of talks on a certain subject that I have since forgotten. He referenced scripture, but did not read from it much. I found out later that he usually chose a certain subject and would speak on that for several successive Sundays. Man, he was a master motivator, which was right up my alley at that particular time. I have to say, I was fired up and excited about being in that church. Not only that, but we were welcomed warmly by many people in the congregation. I guess they could tell we were new. I could see that the people were very faithful Christians.

I think Nancy was kind of surprised when I said, "I think this is the place for us." As time went on, we attended several of that church's functions and began getting acquainted with the people there. We were invited to join a Bible study, which the Catholic church we attended did not offer at the time. In fact, we were eager to experience it. And it was great—for a while.

The pastor approached us one day and said we should be baptized in front of the congregation. I told him that we had both been baptized in the Catholic Church—Nancy as a baby, and me at the age of sixteen. Although he didn't elaborate on the reason, the pastor repeated: "You need to be baptized." That was the end of that particular conversation. Nancy and I discussed this, wondering why he was so adamant, but we temporarily put the subject aside.

As I said, we began attending the Bible study with about ten other people. They called it a "small group." After several sessions, we were really enjoying the discussion and fellowship. It was customary at the end to pray for friends, family members, or just general events in life. If one of my family members were sick, I would request prayer, and we would all do just that. Out of the blue, one of the participants said: "Let's pray for the Catholics, because they think they are Christians, but we know they really aren't." Well, everyone else said, "Amen," and a prayer was offered for the "poor Catholics."

To be very blunt, Nancy and I were totally blindsided and hurt by that occurrence. And they all seemed to absolutely agree. We totally felt deflated and dejected. But neither of us spoke up, I regret to say. We were confused, to say the least. Had we been attending a church that was a lie all our lives? How is it possible that Catholics aren't Christians? Is this why the pastor said we needed to be re-baptized? Were our baptisms not legitimate?

I was bothered, upset, and confused about what was dumped on us that day. That night in bed, all I could do was stare at the ceiling and think about all of this. I got out of bed to get a drink of water and decided to read the Bible for a while. Before returning to bed, I appealed to God in a heartfelt prayer. I told Our Lord that I was distraught and didn't know what to do. I asked for His guidance. As I sat there, I closed my eyes and cleared my mind. What happened next just blew me away. Very clearly, four words entered my mind: "Study the Catholic Church."

There's no doubt in my mind that a clear solution was being offered to me. It never occurred to me to study anything about the Church. And I didn't realize it then, but there was a world of knowledge and material out there that could lead me in the right direction. I didn't know where a study would lead me — to the Catholic Church, or away from it. It was clear to me that I had my marching orders.

I have to tell you, ever since then I have been obsessed with studying the Church and everything related to it. Over the years, I have read many works, both from a Catholic perspective and a non-Catholic perspective. I wanted to know the truth, wherever it led me. I read the history of the Church, which led me to read writings by the Church Fathers, many who actually knew some of the Apostles and were taught the faith by them. Then I went on to study about the Protestant revolt and what the so-called "reformers" were trying to accomplish.

After my initial exhaustive research and study, and a lot of prayer, my conclusion was that the Catholic Church was, without a doubt, the Church Christ founded and was correct on every single aspect of Christianity. I say that because every time I questioned a Catholic teaching, I was able to find compelling, reasonable, and undeniable proof to back up what they taught. And most of that proof came directly from the Bible itself. However, I also discovered that much of what the Church teaches comes from what is called "Sacred Tradition," which was passed down by word of mouth from the Apostles and their successors. That continues to this day. The Holy Spirit is leading us in all truth even now.

By the way, the fact that our knowledge grows and further develops is completely biblical. (Please read 2 Thessalonians 2:15, 1 Corinthians 11:2, and John 21:25.) Not everything Jesus said was recorded in scripture and, again, many of the teachings were passed on from the Apostles to their successors, who did the same.

In Timothy 2:2, Paul told Timothy to entrust what he learned to other faithful men, who would also do that. This Sacred Tradition has continued throughout the history of the Church as new bishops and priests learned from their mentors. This process of ordaining new bishops and priests is termed "apostolic succession."

As you may know, Protestants believe that the Bible alone is the source containing all truth. That concept is known as *sola scriptura*. That concept is actually not biblical in any way.

CHAPTER 3

Home Again

After we returned to the Catholic Church, my thirst for knowledge regarding Christ and His Church intensified. As I gathered more facts and discovered the real truth, my faith skyrocketed even higher. I am very confident and know in my heart that I was inspired by the Holy Spirit to pursue answers regarding the truth of the Church, and no one can convince me otherwise. Nothing else could explain the feeling and desire I still have to learn more about Christianity, which has driven me ever since that message I received in answer to my desperate prayer that night.

Most of my study over the years consisted of reading books, new and old, that could enlighten me more regarding the Catholic Church and its teachings. I have accumulated an extensive library of material. There came a time when I decided to search for a source that could offer me a more structured and methodical way of studying the faith. When I came across an organization called the Marian Catechist Apostolate, it was tailor-made for me. They offered me the opportunity to study at home on my own, and at my own pace. It is a two-year intensive course on everything Catholic.

What was really impressive to me was that the apostolate was founded by Servant of God Father John Hardon. His credentials and reputation as a teacher of the faith were beyond excellent. The course he developed was based on one he put together for Mother Teresa and her Missionaries of Charity at the request of Blessed Pope John Paul II.

Before his death, Father Hardon asked Raymond Leo Cardinal Burke to take over the apostolate as International Director. The two were friends and kindred spirits in the faith, so Cardinal Burke gladly accepted, and he remains our spiritual leader today. I must say, studying this material and being consecrated as a Marian Catechist has been and is a true blessing. It really helped me to fill in the blanks that remained from my personal study. Every year, we catechists have the opportunity to attend "Consecration Weekend" in La Crosse, Wisconsin, at the Shrine of Our Lady of Guadalupe, which Cardinal Burke founded when he was bishop there. Cardinal Burke is always in attendance, offering Holy Mass, giving us guidance, and offering a few talks. It is an outstanding event, and I'm honored to be part of it.

In my journey of faith, I have come to experience Mass in a whole different way. Christ's sacrifice is a stark reality to me, and when I receive the Eucharist, I'm so humbled and blessed because I feel Christ's presence in me. Receiving communion is the most important thing we can do in this life. My whole outlook on life has changed, and my priorities are very different now. Honestly, I'm still amazed at what God has done for me. That "thing" that was missing during my earlier pursuit of "success" is now front and center in my life. I thank Our Lord for blessing me in this way, and in so many other ways.

I know I was called to do what I am doing. I'm happy I answered that call. Sometimes in life we get so busy and caught up that we don't take time to listen to what God might be saying to us. I've come to realize through much prayer and study that we are mainly in this world to love and serve Our Lord. Now I try to look beyond the trappings of this world and focus more on the world to come, which is much more important. After all, it's where we will spend eternity. When you think about it, our existence on earth is relatively short! Both Heaven and Hell are for eternity. We ourselves get to choose our eternal destination.

CHAPTER 4

It's Up to Us

That's right, we all have the opportunity to choose Heaven or Hell. God gave us free will and a mind capable of reason and learning.

Contrary to popular opinion, our purpose on earth is not simply to enjoy ourselves, have fun, and accumulate as much "stuff" as we can. That is very shallow thinking indeed. We have been provided with a divine "rule book" and oral teaching passed down from the beginning. Why is it that many of us don't care to follow those rules and really learn more about what God expects of us?

It seems as though, to many, salvation history is sort of a mythological story. People say they are Christians, but they are not willing to do what is necessary to actually be one. If you don't know the Bible, study the faith, and live according to Christ's teachings, how can you expect to end up in Heaven?

Actually having an intimate friendship with Jesus Christ is absolutely necessary. In order to achieve that, we must have a strong prayer life. The ultimate point I'm trying to get across is that just going to church on Sunday, but not giving God much thought during the week, will not cut it. We have become a self-centered people, relentlessly pursuing the things that we believe make us happy. True happiness can only be achieved by being Christ-centered.

It's time to leave our sphere of ignorance regarding Christ and His Church. It is incumbent on us to take time to read the Bible and study the faith from the heart of the Catholic Church—the Church of Jesus himself. There is so much material out there to explore about the history of the Church. Many of the first Christians wrote things down, and this is available to read if you only pursue it.

Saint Jerome said, "Ignorance of Scripture is ignorance of Christ." Don't settle for just knowing the basics. Believe me, it can make all the difference in your life. I say this as a guy who barely knew the basics for many years. I continue to study and pray and get closer to Christ, and it enriches my life beyond belief. I hope and pray that you will do the same.

CHAPTER 5

The Real Story

Catholics and Protestants have something in common: They are Christians because they love and have faith in Jesus Christ. Even though some Protestant denominations don't think we Catholics are Christians, we don't believe that about them. However, what we know is that all of the thousands of Protestant denominations are not practicing Christianity as Christ taught us. Much is missing in their worship and even in their Bible. This is certainly not the fault of faithful Protestants who were born into families that have worshipped this way for generations. It is unfortunate that they just don't know what they don't know. Also, many misleading myths have been passed on to them about the Catholic Church.

For instance, many say that Catholics "added" books to the Bible. Well, the opposite is actually the truth. Martin Luther, and his cohorts, took seven books out of the Bible because those books taught things contrary to what he wanted to teach in "his version" of Christianity. Luther even wanted to slash out some New Testament books, but he backed off on that because he received opposition from many even in his own ranks.

The books they removed from the Old Testament were read and relied on by Christ and His Apostles, so why then were they removed? Think about that. The complete Catholic Bible existed for about 1200 years before Luther arrived on the scene. It's baffling to me that a man—a Catholic priest no less—would come along and have the temerity to change the inspired Word of God, change the method of worship, reinterpret scripture to his own liking, and get tens of millions of people to follow him; and it continues now. The vast number of faithful Christians that oppose Christ's Church and follow Luther's way not only confounds me, but it saddens me.

Unfortunately, Protestants do not experience the fullness of the Christian faith; they only get some of it. Yes, they love Christ, but they don't receive His real body, blood, soul, and divinity in the Eucharist. To them, communion is a mere symbol. Also, to them, baptism is symbolic and doesn't have much to do with one's salvation. Of course, the Bible says that baptism now saves you (1 Peter 3:21). Whenever they found a new believer, a new Christian, the first thing they did was baptize that person.

Protestants say they rely on the "Bible alone" (*sola scriptura*), but they ignore many very clear verses that say the opposite of what they teach.

I truly believe that if more Protestants actually knew the true Catholic Church, they would come home to it immediately. After all, Jesus pleaded with the Father in prayer that the Church would be one as

He and the Father are one. He even went so far as to say "perfectly one." Please take time to read John 17 and contemplate the meaning of Christ's words. More on this later.

CHAPTER 6

The Fullness of the Faith

Only the Catholic Church offers Christians every-thing they need to assure their salvation. Now, that is not to say that non-Catholic Christians will not reach Heaven. Only God knows the answer to that.

Christ himself instituted the seven sacraments through which we receive His grace; I call it "spiritual power." A combination of our faith and God's grace gives us the best chance of reaching Heaven. Who doesn't want the best chance of attaining something great, especially if that goal is being with God for eter-nity? When the Bible tells us that the path to Heaven is narrow and the one to Hell is wide, it's probably a good idea to do anything and everything possible to please Our Lord. Please pause here and read Matthew 7:13-14, 21-23, and Luke 13:23-24.

To those who are Catholics, realize that you are definitely a member of Christ's one true Church. Also understand that if you are not a faithful Catholic who is obedient to all Church teachings, that makes you a CINO (Catholic in Name Only). In other words, we as Catholics must adhere to all that Christ passed on to the Church. One cannot pick and choose the teachings one likes based on personal preferences. That might work in politics, but it has no place when it comes to the Church.

I'm confident, based on experience, that many so-called Catholics will continue in their errant ways in spite of what I have stated here. How do I know? Because I've been scolded and rebuffed by many people to whom I've gently explained certain Church teachings—as though I was imparting my own personal opinion on the matter. I've been called "judgmental" and told that I must think I'm better than they are. I will continue to defend and teach the truth when given the opportunity. We were commanded by Jesus to do just that.

To any Protestants who might be reading this book, I ask you to do some studying and praying about this matter. It couldn't hurt to look into it, right? Don't just believe everything you've been told by others. I promise you that you will be happy and thankful that you did. We would love for you to be reunited with Christ's Catholic Church.

CHAPTER 7

The Eucharist

Jesus began the formation of His Church when the Twelve Apostles were gathered. The instruction He gave them over the next three years is passed on by the Church until the end of the world.

The most important teaching of Christ occurred about a year before the Last Supper. Although the Apostles didn't entirely grasp what Jesus meant, they chose to trust Him on the subject. What I'm referring to is the "Bread of Life" discourse in John 6:22-71. Before the crucifixion, they would all come to realize that what Jesus would give them, and all Christians, was the opportunity to actually eat His flesh and drink His blood. In this way, He would always be with us, even if we could not actually see Him.

Receiving the Eucharist is an act of total faith and, we believe as Catholics, necessary for salvation. For those non-Catholics who never receive this important teaching, but they love and have faith in Jesus Christ, we believe God will, through His mercy, reconcile with them in the end. It is important to note, however, if one has had this teaching and he or she chooses to reject it, all bets could be off. I would not want to bet my salvation on it. It is very important that you re-read John 6 and also the account of the Last Supper. What else could Jesus have meant? Pray and think hard about His words.

I must say that once I understood the origin and intrinsic nature of the Eucharist, my whole world changed. When I truly understood the grace that one receives when eating the body and blood of Christ, my existence in this world took on a new meaning. I am confident that it will do the same for you.

CHAPTER 8

One Church

Did Jesus Christ intend for there to be one Church united in the faith, which would pass on His teachings? Was Jesus mistaken when He told the Apostles the Holy Spirit would guide the Church in all truth until the end of time? Did Jesus pass His authority on to the Apostles and their successors or not? We Catholics believe He did all of these things.

Yet, our Protestant brethren think the Holy Spirit fell down on the job, and in 1517 a disgruntled priest came to "save" the Church. There are now in excess of 30,000 different Protestant denominations. I will repeat that their beliefs, traditions, and biblical interpretations vary tremendously. Is that what Jesus was praying for in John 17? The obvious answer is absolutely not.

To reiterate, it would be wrong for me to suggest that all of the popes, bishops, priests, and religious have been perfect followers of Christ. There have always been unfaithful individuals both inside and outside of the Church. Christ and the Apostles warned us about future false teachers and the heresy they would attempt to spread. But they also taught us, in no uncertain terms, that "the gates of hell" would never prevail against the Church. Isn't that a good reason to not stray from Christ's one true Church? Also, know that most of the major heresies were begun by bishops and priests. They are not all perfect by any means.

The four marks of the Church are that it is One, Holy, Catholic, and Apostolic. That is what Jesus desired from the beginning. It is imperative that we reunite all Christians back into the Catholic Church and honor Christ's prayer for unity (John 17).

Apostolic Succession

At the behest of Jesus Christ, the Apostles followed His instructions to choose others to be leaders and teachers in the Church, who would in turn choose others to succeed them. The new leaders would always receive comprehensive instruction in the faith. The bishops would lay their hands on them and ordain them.

Again, this process, which continues today, is called "apostolic succession." Those who are ordained in this direct line from the Apostles are legitimate bishops, priests, and deacons, with the authority from Christ himself to teach and provide the holy sacraments to the faithful. Protestant pastors do not have this authority, plain and simple. Ordination is one of the seven sacraments instituted by Jesus himself, by the way.

Peter was the first pope, and the line of popes since then has been unbroken. Yes, I know the title "pope" is not in the Bible. That title was given by the Church itself, which is guided by the Holy Spirit to make such determinations. Pope means "papa" in Italian. However, the fact that Christ chose Peter to lead His Church is really indisputable. The evidence of Peter's primacy and leadership in scripture seems impossible to deny, even though some do. The other Apostles looked to Peter for guidance. It would be instructive and profitable for the reader to pause here and read a few passages from scripture on this subject. I suggest Matthew 16:18-19, Luke 22:32, John 21:17, Acts 2:14, Acts 3:6-7, and Acts 15:7. Also, Peter's name appears in scripture 195 times, which is more than all of the other Apostles combined.

Christ set up the Church's hierarchy from the beginning. Scripture bears this fact out if you only look for it. It's amazing to me that things like this can be sort of skimmed over and ignored. But in many instances they are.

When it comes to biblical interpretation, why is it that in the Protestant world each individual and denomination can interpret a given passage in their own way? Is God's truth solid? Can you have your truth and I mine? When there is a dispute among Christians, who decides the answer? I know that Protestants believe that all of the answers are in the Bible. Well, that just can't be. In fact, the Bible indicates that the opposite is really true.

Of course, the Bible is the inspired Word of God, but that is only part of the picture. Remember, for almost four-hundred years there was no completely compiled New Testament. The teaching of the faith was by word of mouth. Again, we call that Sacred Tradition. Many of the Church Fathers (bishops and priests) wrote extensively about scripture and specific aspects of the faith. That began in the first century. These writings are available for anyone to read. The truth can be found in what they say, in addition to what's in the Bible.

Jesus told the Apostles that "whoever hears you, hears me, and whoever rejects you, rejects me" (See Luke 10:16). That obviously goes for those whom the Apostles ordained, on down the line. What Traditions?

Protestants wrongfully say that Catholics adhere to the "traditions of men," which is against the Bible. Honestly, that is a gross mischaracterization of our beliefs. If the Bible is their sole source of the truth, how can they ignore verses like 1 Corinthians 11:12, 2 Thessalonians 2:15, and 2 Thessalonians 3:6? Read those passages and think about their meaning. Also, Romans 10:17 says that "faith comes from what is heard." The Bible is very "profitable" for Christians, but it doesn't contain everything we need. The combination of faith, scripture, Sacred Tradition, and receiving the sacraments gives us the grace we require as Christians. All of this put together and passed on down through the ages is called the "deposit of faith."

In John 21:25, it is written that basically all that Jesus said and did could not be written down in a book. Much of what is not written has been and is passed on by spoken words.

Jesus gave the Apostles authority, through Him, to baptize new Christians and to teach them the faith. Again, I must repeat that He also told them the Holy Spirit would be with the Church until "the end of the age" (Matthew 28:18-20).

Our Lord also reminded His followers that the Holy Spirit would be with them always to teach and remind them of everything they had learned (John 14:16 and 26).

Furthermore, Saint Paul wrote in 1 Timothy 3:15 that the Church (not just the Bible) is the "pillar and foundation" of the truth. The Church Saint Paul is referring to is the Catholic Church. In Matthew 16:17-19, Jesus not only personally appoints Peter to lead the Church, He stated that the "gates of hell" would never prevail against His Church. In the language of that period, "gates" meant "power."

CHAPTER 9

Our Blessed Mother

One of the hardest things for Protestants to grasp is our love for and devotion to Mary, the Mother of Our Lord. To them, she was merely an earthly vessel through which our Savior would enter the world. Basically, the only time Mary is referenced in non-Catholic Christian churches is during Christmas time.

I find this incredible and bewildering on many levels. How can any Christian church pay so little attention to the woman Christ himself chose to be His earthly mother? I just don't get that.

When the angel appeared to the young woman, Mary, did he say something like: "Hello, young lady. Your body will be used to bring a baby into this world, and then you can just go on about your business."

Well, not quite. Mary was addressed by Gabriel in a most reverent way, saying this: "Hail, full of grace… you have found favor with God." After hearing that she would bear the Son of God in her womb, she joyfully and reverently accepted, calling herself "the handmaid of the Lord."

In case you missed it, the angel said Mary was "full of grace." Grace was not fully actualized for mankind until Christ came and instituted the sacraments for the benefit of our souls and the salvation thereof. Mary was the only human being to be afforded grace before Jesus's birth. That is why the Church has determined, with the help of the Holy Spirit, that Mary was conceived and born sinless. So when Mary was conceived in her mother's womb, that is called the "Immaculate Conception." Only a completely purified woman was worthy enough to become the Mother of God on earth.

When Mary's cousin, Elizabeth, who was pregnant with John the Baptist, saw Mary, the baby in Elizabeth's womb leapt at the presence of Jesus within Mary. Elizabeth proclaimed: "Blessed are you among women...." Mary responded that "henceforth, all generations will call me blessed...."

Based on those verses alone, wouldn't you agree that Mary is very special indeed? How can anyone who calls himself or herself a Christian deny that? Anyone claiming to be a "Bible Christian," who doesn't perceive Mary's unique role, should re-read these verses and pray about it. Also consider the commandment "Honor thy father and thy mother." Would the Author of that commandment do anything less? I certainly don't believe so.

The Church teaches that Mary was special, and she is even more special in Heaven. There have been several Marian apparitions, confirmed by the Church, where Our Blessed Mother warns us and gives us instructions in order to lead us to her Son. When we ask in prayer for her intercession, she hears us, and it pleases Jesus.

They Pray to the Saints

This is another subject that confuses me when it comes to Protestant thinking. I've heard countless non-Catholics say to people: "Please pray for me," or "pray for so and so, who is sick." Yet, they find it strange when we pray to a saint to ask for his/her intercession or prayers. Do the saints stop being members of Christ's Church when they die? No, they are still our brothers and sisters in Christ in Heaven. The only difference is that they are now with Our Lord and are even better able to help us. We Catholics realize that only God can answer prayers, but it is also fruitful to appeal to those who can add their prayers to ours—especially the saints in Heaven. Prayers are very, very powerful.

They Pray to Statues

I find it insulting and silly to have to address this claim by many non-Catholics, but here I go. When one looks at a photo of a deceased family member, what is he/she doing? Bringing to mind the person in the photo, remembering a special day with that person, or another fond memory. The concept of praying before a statue of the Virgin Mary, for example, or a great champion of the faith, is the same thing. It puts us in mind of that special person. Sacred art and statues remind us of Christ and those who have helped spread the faith throughout history. If that doesn't satisfy people who find Catholic statues and art offensive, well, I just give up.

They Pray for the Dead

This subject would be easier to understand for Protestants if Martin Luther hadn't decided to strike certain Old Testament books from "his" Bible. I wonder why he did that. Oh, well, anyway, you can read 2 Maccabees 12:44-46, which references atonement for the dead. There are several references to what we call "Purgatory" in both the Old Testament and New Testament. Saint Paul prays for a deceased friend of his named Onesiphorus (See 2 Timothy 1:16-18).

If there is nothing we can do to help the dead, why would Paul do that? I respectfully ask our Protestant brothers and sisters to take a fresh look at this subject.

CHAPTER 10

How Are We Saved?

The question of how we are saved has been in dispute ever since the Protestant revolt. Up until that unfortunate time in the Church's history, Christians knew that we were saved by, first, our baptism. (See 1 Peter 3:21, Titus 3:5, and Acts 122:16.) But that's not the end of it. If we are not obedient to the Lord's commandments, our salvation can be lost. Consequently, it's a combination of baptism, faith, plus works — yes, "works" — that will get us to Heaven. (Please read James 2:24-26, Matthew 19:16-17, and 1 Corinthians 13:2).

Protestants who insist that they believe the Bible alone (*sola scriptura*) is their sole guide somehow miss these important verses. According to non-Catholic Christians, you are saved forever by praying what they call the "sinner's prayer," accepting Jesus Christ as their "personal" Lord and Savior. Once you perform that act, you are good to go, no matter what you do or don't do in your life. The big problem with this "way to salvation" is that it is nowhere to be found in the Bible, which they say has all the authority. How can that be?

One cannot claim absolute adherence to scripture and then cherry-pick what he or she will believe.

Bible Alone?

Let's examine more closely this doctrine of *sola scriptura* (Bible alone). If one studies the early Church through the writings of the Church Fathers, and reads several New Testament verses, reason alone would tell him or her that *sola scriptura* is actually non-biblical. Yet, unbelievably, many still cling to this errant doctrine.

Saint Paul wrote to the Thessalonians that they should hold fast to the traditions they were taught, whether oral or by letter (See 2 Thessalonians 3:6). Saint Paul also instructed Timothy to entrust what he heard to other faithful men (See 2 Timothy 2:2).

Never once did Jesus tell the Apostles to go write down what I've taught you. What He did say was to go and make disciples of all nations, teaching them to observe His commandments (See Matthew 28:18-20).

Remember, there was no complete New Testament until almost AD 400. To be clear, we Catholics do believe the Bible is the inspired Word of God, and it is very profitable in our lives. However, it is not, and was not meant to be, everything we need to live a truly Christian life. Following the teachings of the Bible, having faith, doing good works, and adhering to Sacred Tradition will put us on the "narrow path" to Heaven. Yes, the Bible seems to indicate that more people will go to Hell than to Heaven. Many people doubt that.

CHAPTER 11

Is There a Hell?

For some reason that I cannot fathom, many people have come to believe that Hell doesn't really exist. We don't hear much about it in churches anymore. It is said that God is all-loving and merciful, and that He would not "send" anyone to Hell. Well, that's all true. We actually choose our own destination.

Unfortunately, even some Catholic bishops and priests have jumped on this "reasonable hope that all people are saved" bandwagon. Just compare murderers like Stalin and Hitler to great saints like Peter and Paul; Do they all deserve the same reward on Judgment Day? Albeit a deathbed confession and repentance could actually save people like them. Forgiveness is always available, which reflects the real love and mercy of Our Lord. But remember, God is also just.

Based on scripture, is it reasonable to assume that all people will be saved in the end? As a sample from several references to damnation in scripture, take some time and read Isaiah 33:14-16, Matthew 25:41-46, and 2 Thessalonians 1:6-9. Words describing Hell came directly out of the mouth of Our Lord. Who can dispute that? But some do, unbelievably.

If Hell doesn't exist, why follow Christ's teachings at all? We should be able to do anything and live however we want. Why do we have the Ten Commandments if we don't really need to follow them?

Look, anyone with an average intellect and the ability to reason should be able to figure this out. How is it that even some bishops, priests, and highly educated theologians buy into this malarkey? I think that sometimes people try to mold God into what they want Him to be; that way, they can lessen the severity of sin and we can all get away with more. That would make life much easier, and we could all have so much more fun.

Except that's not what the Bible and Sacred Tradition teach us. Why did Jesus Christ go through the crucifixion to pay for our sins if it wasn't necessary? The instructions for living a Christian life must be optional, because we're all going to end up in the same place anyway, right? Wrong! Can you tell that this kind of thinking frustrates me? Let's move on.

Chapter 12

The Real Presence

When Jesus first spoke to a large group of followers (including the Apostles) saying they will have to eat His body and drink His blood in order to have life in them, it caused a huge problem. As these people discussed what they were told, many decided to leave Jesus. They could not and would not accept what Our Lord taught, believing He was referring to what amounted to cannibalism.

Normally, when one believes he is misunderstood, he will usually further explain or clarify what he means. In fact, Jesus did just that many times in biblical accounts. But in this case, He did not call anyone back and attempt to re-explain or clarify anything He said. Instead, He turned to Peter and the other Apostles and asked if they would also leave Him. Of course, they stayed with Our Lord because of their deep faith in Him and belief in what they were learning. They knew in their hearts that Jesus meant exactly what He said and was not speaking symbolically in any way. They trusted that as time progressed they would more fully understand His words.

As you read John 6, you can see that Jesus said the same thing in several different ways; He wasn't speaking ambiguously at all. At the Last Supper, the Apostles would receive a full understanding of what their Lord told them on that day. They now knew that they and everyone throughout time would be able to actually receive Jesus in the bread and wine because of the divine miracle Christ instituted. Even though Jesus would not be visible to us until His return, He would be with us, and within us, through the Holy Eucharist.

Even now, people are leaving Jesus because of His declaration on that day so long ago. These people are ex-Catholics who don't agree with the Church's teaching, Protestants, and every non-Christian. Many Catholics never really believed or understood the doctrine of the Real Presence of Our Lord in the Eucharist. Sadly, I must admit to being in that camp myself for many years. I am eternally thankful that my eyes were opened to the truth.

The Truth

I now know that if we want to know the truth about anything, we must seek it on our own. One must desire the truth. In my own professional and business life, I figured that concept out at a young age. But when it came to the most important thing of all—my salvation—I just didn't think much about it. Why are we human beings like that? We always look for something that will benefit us, right? We like to get an advantage over others, right? The best deal on a new car makes us happy, right? You can see where I'm going with this discourse. Human beings are naturally self-absorbed, self-centered, and we all have an inclination toward sin. That inclination is known as "concupiscence." We can thank Adam and Eve for the original sin that every one of us—except Our Blessed Mother—is born with.

Christ allows Satan to roam the earth seeking the ruin of souls, but He gives us all the spiritual weapons we need to resist the devil's instigations, or temptations. Those weapons are the sacraments that we can get only from the Catholic Church. Through these sacraments, we receive an abundance of grace directly from God. Jesus Christ himself instituted every one of these sacraments. Yes, you can find it all in the Bible. A review of the seven sacraments is always profitable just in case we forgot what Jesus left us. Many Catholics never really grasp the importance of the sacraments because they were not taught doctrine properly. Unfortunately, teaching of the faith has been very weak in the last fifty years or so.

CHAPTER 13

The Sacraments

Baptism

First, we'll talk about baptism. Baptism saves us
(1 Peter 3:21). Original sin is wiped away when
we are baptized, which is necessary for our salvation.
Everywhere in the New Testament, when a person
becomes a believer, he or she is baptized immediately.
Many times whole families were baptized together,
including babies, in the early days of Christianity. It is
unbiblical to not baptize a baby.

Many Protestant denominations don't believe
babies should be baptized, and that they should wait
until they are old enough to understand and accept
baptism, which is only symbolic to them. Where is that
in the Bible? It's not there! That is a dangerous belief
on their part. Of course, some other denominations
are willing to baptize infants. But not one Protestant
denomination that I know of believes baptism saves us.
But that IS in the Bible. Go figure.

The Catholic Church recognizes baptisms in any
Christian church, upon sufficient investigation, if the
minister had a proper intention and it is done with the

water flowing across the forehead, or by submersion, and these words are spoken: "I baptize you in the name of the Father, and of the Son, and of the Holy Spirit." If a Protestant converts to the Catholic Church and was properly baptized, a re-baptism is not necessary. As stated before, some Protestant denominations don't afford Catholic converts to Protestantism the same courtesy. If you were properly baptized, you are actually considered a member of the Catholic Church.

Confession (Reconciliation)

This sacrament is extremely important in the lives of Christians. Yet, even many Catholics have concluded that it's not necessary to tell a priest our sins. Somewhere along the line, the Church's teaching on confession has been sort of left behind, ignored. Again, many blame this on the poor catechesis (teaching) over the last several years. I agree wholeheartedly with that conclusion. The hard teachings have been, and are still being, watered down.

As a young man who was a "victim" of poor catechesis, I bought into the Protestant idea that we just need to talk to God directly and express sorrow for our sins. Well, that's true, and there's nothing wrong with talking to Our Lord, that's for sure. But Jesus himself instituted the sacrament of confession. Please pause here and read John 20:21-23 and Matthew 18:18. You will see that Jesus most definitely gave the Apostles, and thereby their successors, the authority to forgive sins. When priests administer confession, they are acting "*In Persona Christi*," or in the person of Christ, on Christ's behalf.

For over thirty years, I did not go to confession. I thank Our Lord that I was led back to the truth. I ask all Catholics, who may be doing what I did, to please come back to confession (reconciliation). It is necessary, my brothers and sisters, if you want to have the fullness of the faith. And I must say that I was warmly welcomed by the priest who heard my very lengthy confession after being away for so long. He was very patient, helpful, understanding, and kind.

Here's a little advice to those who wish to return to this sacrament: Get a hold of something called an "Examination of Conscience." It will help bring to mind sins you may have forgotten. Your church will have a copy.

Sit down with pen and paper and review your life in your mind. Jot down your sins as they come to you. Take the list with you to confession. Also take a copy of the Act of Contrition, because if you're like me, I forgot how it went after all those years.

Very important: Make an appointment with a priest for your confession. That way, you won't have to hurry and you won't hold up the line at the confessional. Believe me, the priest, and anyone waiting in line, will greatly appreciate this.

Remember that you are talking to Jesus through His ordained priest. You must be truly sorry for your offenses in order to receive forgiveness. If you remember another sin after this confession, make a note of it and confess it the next time. I can tell you from personal experience, it's not as difficult as you may perceive it to be. If you are humble and have true contrition, Christ, through the priest, is eager to forgive whatever sins you have. After all, He is your loving Father.

Eucharist

This sacrament is at the center of our faith as Catholics. If you don't believe that the host and wine you consume at Mass is actually (not symbolically) the body, blood, soul, and divinity of Our Lord Jesus Christ, you are not Catholic and should not be receiving communion. If you are receiving the Eucharist and are not in a state of grace, you are making a grave error. You must confess your mortal sins with true contrition (remorse) before receiving Christ in the Eucharist. Otherwise, you profane the Lord and you don't obtain the sought-after grace. In other words, you are offending God, adding sin to sin.

I realize these are very blunt statements. We live in a world where the truth is obscured and sugarcoated in order to not offend people. But we must understand that when it comes to the salvation of our souls, the truth should be spoken plainly. There is absolutely nothing in this world that is more important.

This truth will only be ignored at our peril. I urge and implore you to study your faith and learn the most important facts of all! We are only pilgrims on a short voyage toward a destination of our own choosing. That place will either be one of constant beauty, peace, and love, or one of eternal pain and despair.

Please read John 6 once again, which is Our Lord's Bread of Life discourse. He explains clearly the Catholic teaching on the Real Presence of Jesus in the bread and wine we consume at Mass. Then, re-read the account of the Last Supper.

Understanding the Eucharist is essential to all Catholics, and it is something our non-Catholic brothers and sisters need to seriously and prayerfully revisit. When Jesus states in no uncertain terms that "unless you eat the flesh of the Son of Man, and drink His blood, you do not have life within you," it is all-important that we believe Him and do it.

Another thing many Catholics don't know is that the entire presence of Jesus (body, blood, soul, and divinity) is in both the bread and wine. So that one can receive just the bread, or just the wine, or both. Personally, I usually just receive the host (bread). Also, I choose to receive communion on the tongue, not in the hand. Both receiving on the tongue and in the hand are acceptable these days in the Church. There is a story behind that situation, but I will leave that for another time and place.

Confirmation

The three sacraments of initiation are baptism, confirmation, and the Holy Eucharist. As we should know, baptism gives us a share in the divine life, makes us children of God. Confirmation completes our initiation as members of Christ's Church.

Recently, I asked several Catholics what their understanding of confirmation was. More often than not, they told me it was when a young Catholic was old enough to choose for himself or herself to be a Christian. Many were under the impression that it was similar to the Protestant doctrine of "accepting Christ as your personal savior." Wrong.

First of all, God chose us; we don't simply "accept" Him. As Christians, we must believe His Word, follow His commandments, and strive for holiness. The sacraments Christ initiated provide us with the grace, or spiritual power, to avoid sin. Confirmation increases our grace in this regard, makes us soldiers of Christ. In other words, confirmation is yet another gift from God. It is not something that we just "accept"; it is freely given to us from our Creator. The blessings and gifts of the Holy Spirit become greater in confirmation; in other words, we are infused more abundantly with the Holy Spirit. The increased presence of the Spirit received in confirmation strengthens our minds and hearts by the Divine Wisdom and gives us courage and fortitude to avoid sin and do God's will in our lives. The key is to desire God's will in all things. If we do, He will give us the ability to endure all of the difficulties we encounter while in this world.

Many of us don't realize it, but the Apostles were confirmed on Pentecost Sunday when the Holy Spirit filled their hearts and souls so that they could go forth unafraid and proclaim the Gospel of the Lord. When we are confirmed, we receive a share of those same graces.

We must rely on the Holy Spirit who dwells within us, trusting that He will guide us and protect us. It is important to pray often and act on the inspirations we receive from the Holy Spirit. When we pray and ask for help or direction, we will get it in one form or another.

Sometimes a prayer is not answered in the way we want or expect, but there's always an answer. Think about it.

Matrimony

In today's confusing world, the sacrament of marriage is being ravaged, distorted, and profaned. Beginning in the first book of the Bible, marriage is defined as the union of a man and woman who love one another, have children, and live a family life in accordance with God's law.

Jesus Christ elevated the act of marriage to be a sacrament. In a Christian marriage, Christ is the essential third partner through whom comes special graces. The dignity of marriage and family is under attack now more than at any other time in human history.

Some of the many challenges to marriage as devised by God are: divorce, same-sex "marriage," hedonism/selfishness, and contraception. Many countries, including the United States, are now promoting and extolling the "virtues" of the marriage of same-sex couples. According to the Word of God, men and women were created to complement each other, love one another, and procreate. Same-sex unions contradict God's divine purpose for His creation.

For the life of me, I cannot understand why so many self-proclaimed Christians now wholeheartedly approve of the gay and lesbian lifestyle, and see nothing wrong with them getting "married." Either these same-sex marriage advocates are ignorant of the Bible and Church teachings on the subject, or they just reject it altogether. I won't go into great detail about why the act of homosexuality is such a grave sin. I will leave it up to you the reader to pursue the truth. I recommend that you begin by reading Genesis 19:1-11 and Leviticus 18:22 and 20:13 in the Old Testament. Then read 1 Corinthians 6:9-10, Romans 1:18-32, and 1 Timothy 1:3-11, in the New Testament.

The people in this world with same-sex attraction are indeed carrying a heavy burden. Other types of burdens also exist in this world, such as sickness and disease, extreme poverty, great oppression, and many, many other afflictions. As Christians, we are called to carry our burdens willingly and offer them up to God in faith. We are to avoid sin that comes as a result of our burdens and temptations. We must avail ourselves of the sacraments to help us in our weakness.

Remember, we are here on earth for what is really a short time. What we do while on this earthly pilgrimage determines our eternal destination. I urge same-sex attracted people to seek help in the Church, and to be guided by the Word of God. Like all of us, they must avoid sinful acts in order to reach Heaven in the end.

True Christians are to love homosexuals and help them when possible. True love and charity moves us to help them avoid grave sin. It has become commonplace to refer to Christians who are against same-sex marriage as being hateful, prejudiced, and politically incorrect. But the people who think they are being loving and accepting of individuals who are "different" are leading them down the path of destruction. It's a crazy, mixed-up world, which is becoming harder and harder to navigate. Let's rely on God, and all will end up well. We can't fall into the trap of political correctness at the expense of Christ's and the Church's moral teachings.

As Christians, we must stand up for our moral values at all costs.

I realize that same-sex marriage is being "legalized" everywhere now. We are to follow our man-made laws, yes, unless they blatantly defy the Word of God. Then we need to stand up for religious freedom and the natural law of God. We need not accept and buckle to anything and everything that is being promoted as "good." After all, we are the Church Militant here on earth, and we need to fight against evil in all its forms.

One last regrettable thing must be mentioned. There are many cardinals, bishops, priests, and nuns within the Church who actually support active homosexuals and same-sex marriage. Indeed, many of them are gay or lesbian themselves. Unfortunately, this has been proven over and over, so I'm not saying anything that's not well-known. They are actually attempting to change the unchangeable teachings of Christ and the Church.

Either these ordained men and religious women never had faith, or they have lost it somewhere along the line. To be sure, we will all be held to account for our actions in this life when we die. I daresay that bishops, priests, and nuns will probably be held to a higher standard before Our Lord. They are supposed to be leading souls to Heaven, not doing the opposite. I pray every day for the lost Church leaders, and I hope you will do the same. There's always time to repent of the evil they are doing.

Back to marriage briefly. Husbands and wives are to share their thoughts and affections with one another. The unique roles of both father and mother are extremely important to the proper development of their children. It is the important vocation of parents to teach the faith to their children, so that they will know it and pass it on to their own children. Saint John Paul II said, "The future of humanity passes by way of the family."

Holy Orders

I learned in my studies over the years something that people may not realize, which is this: Without the sacrament of Holy Orders, there would be no Christianity, and thus, no Catholic Church. Christ instituted Holy Orders to continue His mission here in this world.

Through ordained priests, we receive leadership in the Church, reconciliation, anointing of the sick, and most important, the Holy Eucharist and the Mass. Our parish priests are to carry out the redemptive work of Christ and strive to bring souls to Heaven.

Holy Orders began with the Apostles and have continued within the Catholic Church in an unbroken, uninterrupted, and continuous manner. Only priests — Catholic priests — in this unbroken chain of ordained men can consecrate the Eucharist and offer the Sacrifice of the Mass. Only ordained priests can forgive our sins through Christ, because the Lord gave the Apostles this ability personally (See John 20:21-23).

At this point, I am compelled to tell my Protestant brothers and sisters that you simply don't have this all-important blessing at your service, and your ministers cannot offer you the most important sacrament that Christ gave us. Martin Luther and the other so-called "reformers" chose to ignore the Lord's words and rejected this very, very important sacrament. Consider that these were the beliefs of all Church bishops and priests from the beginning—until the year 1517, when the "reformation" began. That is very strong evidence that the Catholic Church had it right all along, wouldn't you say?

Why would Luther, a Catholic priest at the time, choose to all of a sudden ignore scripture and Church teaching? Many believe that he lost his faith for some reason. Yes, there were abuses of the faith going on in the Church, as there was all along. But for Luther to believe that he could mold the teachings of the faith to his liking was a grave mistake on his part. Once again, Christ set up the Church and taught the Apostles how and what to pass on, telling them that the Holy Spirit would guide them until the end of the world. To me, it's very reasonable to deduce that one human being—a priest no less—cannot change what Christ put in place. Yet, millions in this world still follow and believe the heresy that Luther and the other false teachers of that time brought forth.

Anointing of the Sick

This sacrament goes back to the very early days of the Church. It is also referred to as "extreme unction." Most Catholics over the years have heard this practice called "last rites," which is performed on a person at the time just prior to his or her death.

The fact is that any person of any age with a serious illness can be anointed. Even though you won't see it in the New Testament explicitly, Sacred Tradition reveals to us that this sacrament dates back to Christianity's early days.

Anointing of the sick is essential because of its spiritual effects. It strengthens the supernatural life of the soul and restores sanctifying grace to a sinful person. It is best when the person being anointed is truly sorry for his or her sins. Having a complete trust and confidence in God's love and mercy is the best disposition to have when being anointed. Anointing can remove penalty for sin and lessen temporal punishment in Purgatory.

Anointing can even heal the body, if it is God's will. It has happened in many cases over the centuries. Christ healed many during His earthly ministry. After all, God is the one who ultimately effectuates this sacrament, along with all the other sacraments. Faith in Him and belief in the sacraments given to us can lead to miracles even now. Many instances of healing have happened at places like Lourdes, Guadalupe, and Fatima.

Jesus Christ left us a Church that contains all of the channels of grace that strengthen our souls and give us the best chance of reaching Heaven when we pass on from this world. We, as Christians, should fully accept and receive all of the graces the Lord has granted us. Non-Catholics are at a severe disadvantage in their journey toward eternity in Heaven. They simply do not have the fullness of the Christian faith. I strongly urge my Protestant brothers and sisters to pray about this and seek the truth by doing your own study. I pray that this book can help you along the way, and that you will consider coming home to Christ's Catholic Church.

CHAPTER 14

The Road to Heaven

In addition to the Old Testament, Christ came to demonstrate to us God's desire for our eternal life. He taught us that we must live in obedience to the Ten Commandments (also referred to as the Decalogue). He brought forth the Beatitudes to clarify and further instruct us.

In the Sermon on the Mount, Christ taught how Christians are to live and behave. In the fifth, sixth, and seventh chapters of Matthew, Christian morality is laid out for us. Our Lord also used the power of parables, or stories, to teach us important lessons.

Jesus is the model that we must strive to copy in our daily lives. Of course, as weak, sinful human beings, we will never reach His level of perfection on our own. But if we put our trust and faith in Him and the Catholic Church, and participate in the sacraments, we can look forward to spending eternity with God in paradise. That should be the main focus and goal in our lives while in this world. Everything else really should pale in comparison.

We've all heard the profound philosophical question: What is the meaning of life? Many have concluded that the answer is to get as much pleasure and stuff as they can while they are here on earth, and if they are just "good people," they will make it to Heaven—if they actually believe there is a Heaven! That kind of thinking is very shallow indeed.

What we as Christians should already realize is that our purpose here is to know, love, and serve Our Lord. We are on a journey during which we are to seek the truth about our existence. We have been provided with the ultimate "rule book," a Holy Church, and the grace we need from the sacraments. Living according to those rules is what will get us to where we want to go in the end.

The Road to Hell

One of the quotes of Our Lord is somewhat telling regarding Heaven and Hell. This one is found in Matthew 7:13:

Enter by the narrow gate; for the gate is wide and the way is easy that leads to destruction, and those who enter by it are many. For the gate is narrow and the way is hard that leads to life, and those who find it are few.

It is the conclusion of many Church Fathers and theologians that this and other parts of scripture tell us clearly that more people will go to Hell than to Heaven. Their argument is very compelling and, to me, believable.

Just declaring oneself to be a Christian and being a relatively good person does not rise to the level of what is necessary for salvation. Jesus made this point in Matthew 7:21-23 in the following way:

> Not everyone who says to me, "Lord, Lord," shall enter the Kingdom of Heaven, but only he who does the will of my Father who is in Heaven. On that day many will say to me, "Lord, Lord, did we not prophesy in your name, and cast out demons in your name, and do many mighty works in your name?" And then will I declare to them, "I never knew you; depart from me, you evildoers."

We as Catholic Christians would be wise to constantly reconsider and re-examine just what we are doing to achieve salvation.

First, do we have an adequate prayer life? It is essential to pray daily.

Are we focusing on doing God's will by following His commandments?

Are we availing ourselves of all of the sacraments He has provided us, which give us the spiritual protection we need in order to avoid sin?

Do we believe and follow all of the teachings of Christ's Catholic Church, or do we pick and choose the ones that suit us?

Another important point to make is that we should not get involved in Church-related programs and activities for the wrong reasons. For instance, joining the Knights of Columbus, parish council, or becoming an extraordinary minister for purely social or self-serving reasons totally misses the point. Unless what we do is for God's greater glory and is to serve Him, we are spinning our wheels, so to speak. If we are doing "good" deeds so that people will respect us and praise us, we are making a serious mistake. One can tell himself or herself that "I do this for God"; but unless that is truly in your heart, you only deceive yourself.

In my personal experience, I find it very difficult to correct someone, or oppose something that is against Church teaching. Doing so—no matter how respectfully or gently—can cause you grief, believe me. Doing so has put me at odds with some family, friends, and even priests. But we are called and obligated to do no less as Christians. If we can rely on Church teachings and scripture to back us up, we should not hesitate to voice the truth. Again, this must be done respectfully and gently. Sometimes my weak human nature kicks in, and I have a little trouble with the being "gentle" part, and my Irish temper rears its ugly head. But the point is that we need to speak the truth and advocate for Christ and His Church. We will always risk the chance that we will be called "judgmental" or acting "greater than thou." So, again, we must make sure we are on solid ground and are armed with proof from the Bible and the Catechism. Good luck! I'll pray for you and you pray for me.

In this age of very weak catechesis, I venture to say that most Catholics know little of their faith. Worse yet, many refuse to believe or follow the actual Church teachings. We cannot mold the faith to our own liking and expect to achieve salvation. I believe that's what Jesus was referring to in the earlier quote from Matthew 7:21-23. Please read it again.

What Are Your Influences?

As Catholics, we are exposed to many ideas and teachings claiming to be in agreement with the Church. I have learned to look very closely at books and programs that are readily available.

When considering a book claiming to have Catholic content, one suggestion I have is to see if it contains a *nihil obstat* and an *imprimatur*, which will be in the front of the book. These designations indicate that the book has been determined to be free of doctrinal error. Now, that does not mean that every book without these designations is bad or wrong, and for some reason it's getting harder to obtain these stamps of approval. My own diocese doesn't even offer the ability to seek their opinion. When you read something that puts a question in your mind, always consult the Catechism and the Bible.

Your best defense against bad and false teaching is to know your faith well. That will make it easy to weed out the bad information you may encounter.

Unfortunately, there are programs held in many dioceses and individual churches that are simply not Catholic. Many sound nice and religious, but they leave out some of the most important aspects of Church teachings. Beware of watered-down Christian programs! If a certain program leaves out topics such as the sacraments—especially the Eucharist—you should probably steer clear of it. In all likelihood, it's more Protestant than anything else. For some reason some bishops and priests think programs that totally lack Catholic teaching, offering meals and feel-good techniques, will help them retain Catholics and bring non-Catholics into their Church. However, the statistics show just the opposite is true. Many Catholics end up thinking that all Christian churches and "denominations" are alike, so why remain Catholic, right?

We all need to realize that the Catholic Church is very unique because Christ made it that way. The sacraments are not something to be skimmed over and forgotten! And we don't have to change our music to Protestant-like, stand-up-and-clap-your-hands music. Our old hymns and Gregorian chants are absolutely beautiful and have a holiness about them. This is a subject that gets me going all the time, but I'll leave it at that for now.

CHAPTER 15

Angels

We each have a guardian angel that protects us in many ways during our sojourn through this world. We should acknowledge them and thank them often. Several books on angels are available for all to read.

I have heard some Catholics say things like, "I think my deceased sister/brother/mother/father is now my guardian angel." In fact, deceased human beings are either in Heaven, Hell, or Purgatory. Like us, angels are separately created beings with immortal souls.

Good angels inhabit Heaven and the earth. Yes, they are among us. Bad angels are also here among us. God has sent His angels to earth as messengers and protectors from the very beginning.

Satan and his demon angels seek to destroy souls and ruin our chance of salvation. The easiest way to let that happen to us is to not cooperate with the will of God and not follow His commandments. If we indulge in evil things and ignore what Christ taught us, we become easy prey for Satan and his bad angels. One may think he or she has a great life on this earth, while doing many depraved things. That is very shallow and dangerous thinking indeed. After all, I repeat, we are here for one main purpose, which is to love and serve Our Lord, and we are not here long. And what we do now will determine where we spend eternity—which is a long, long time! Let that sink in for a few minutes, and it might even change your game plan.

Someone once told me that if we were handed a million dollars every Sunday as we entered the church for Mass, everyone would attend all the time. Of course, right? The lines would be out the door and around the block, and more churches would have to be built. But since we can "only" get salvation and eternal happiness with God by going every Sunday and following the commandments, many people skip Mass to sleep in or do something else. That's a little ironic, isn't it?

I don't think most people would actually choose Hell over Heaven, but we get so caught up in the trappings of this world that it's easy to forget what awaits us in Heaven for eternity. But in order to reach Heaven, we need to follow the rules set out by Christ and His One, Holy, Catholic, and Apostolic Church. Question: Are you willing to do that?

Demons

Like I already mentioned, both good angels and bad angels (demons) are with us on earth. When we go about our daily lives without God and the Church as our number one priority, we open ourselves up to being influenced by the demons. They are real and they want your soul. Demons place temptations to sin before us on behalf of Satan, and they make evil look desirable. Without the armor of God, we are easy prey for them.

In cases where people involve themselves in things such as the occult, atheism, energy healing, yoga, ouija board, fascination with ghosts, witches, movies highlighting the dark arts, and other bad spiritual habits, the door is left open for demons to enter their lives in a strong way. Also, going to palm readers and psychics is condemned by the Church. Believe me, these are not just "harmless" actions, as many believe.

It is very important to know and understand the Church's teachings regarding these dangerous actions, or practices. Again, many Catholics actually believe these things to be harmless. But the fact is that they could prove to be very damaging to your soul. We have come to accept many things in our modern culture that can severely hinder our ability to reach Heaven in the end.

I'm not an expert, by any means, in the area of demonic possession and exorcism, but I've studied sufficiently to know that it's a reality. There are many resources on this subject if one is inclined to look into it.

I mentioned the "armor" of God. Spiritual protection is given to us through faith, prayer, attending Mass, receiving grace through the sacraments, being obedient to all Church teachings, and avoiding all bad spiritual actions. One of the most powerful weapons we possess is the rosary. Many Catholics, sadly, have never prayed the rosary and may not even own rosary beads. I myself thought that only old women used rosary beads. After all, we have all seen these women holding them in Church and on television shows. I regret not using this powerful tool for so long, which was given to us by

Our Lady herself. It is a wonderful meditation on Our Lord's life, ministry, and His death, which was for all of us.

I urge everyone to learn and study about how the rosary came about, and learn what the different mysteries mean. I say to Catholic men that this form of prayer is not just for women. They even make military rosaries and other types that have a more manly design. My favorite is made of special Irish marble; the beads are larger and square, with a bigger crucifix. My point is that we have to put aside our old, ignorant ideas and preconceived notions. The rosary is now a great blessing in my life, and I'm positive you will feel the same. There is a war going on—a spiritual war—and we all need to get in the fight for our souls, those of our loved ones, and all Christians. Again, the rosary is a very powerful weapon, so use it!

CHAPTER 16

The Holy Spirit

There is some confusion, it seems, about the subject of the Holy Spirit's role. We know that the Holy Spirit is the Third Person of the Trinity. As the Church teaches, the Father, Son, and the Holy Spirit are three distinct persons with one divine nature. We say in our Nicene Creed that the Holy Spirit proceeds from both the Father and the Son.

At the Last Supper, Christ told the Apostles that the Father will send "another Advocate" to be with them forever, which meant until the end of time. That being the case, He meant that the Spirit would guide the Church until He returns. From that, it follows that the Church and Christ's teaching would remain in place forever. We have discussed in previous chapters the unity Christ desired from the beginning.

Many of my Protestant friends believe that when they read a Bible passage, the Holy Spirit will reveal its meaning to them. Some also say it can have a different meaning to someone else. A pastor of one Protestant denomination might interpret a passage one way, while another across town will interpret it another way; both claiming guidance by the Holy Spirit. The truth is that the Holy Spirit guides the ordained bishops and priests of the Church Jesus founded with Peter and the other Apostles, which is the Catholic Church. The teaching office, or entity, if you will, is called the Magisterium, which is made up of the pope and bishops. They protect and pass on the immutable, non-negotiable teachings of Christ and the Church as they will always be and have always been.

Many Catholics—including some bishops and priests, apparently—have the mistaken idea that Church teachings can be changed because modern society and culture dictate "new" needs and morals. That is a very grave mistake. We cannot alter what is divine, what Christ has taught us.

Times may change, science may reveal some things (not all good), and we may think of ourselves as modern, different, and self-sufficient. The things of this world are fleeting and superficial. Anything that is revealed to us that is good comes from God, including scientific breakthroughs that help us. Ultimately, we need to concern ourselves with where we will spend eternity, and we should focus more on the supernatural, not the natural world. Without God, we can do nothing—nothing!

The grace we receive from the sacraments comes to us through the Holy Spirit. With that grace, He enlightens us and gives us the will and spiritual strength to fight the temptation of the devil and his demons.

We know, through the Church, that there are seven special gifts of the Holy Spirit. These gifts enable us to practice the virtues of faith, hope, and charity in our lives.

First, the gift of Wisdom helps us to desire the truth of what God has revealed to us. It also helps us to rely on our faith in all matters.

Second is the gift of Understanding. When we seek the truth in faith, it will be revealed to us. Too many people avoid the truth, almost willingly, and remain blind to it, instead relying on what they hear and see in popular culture and politics in this secular world. Big, big mistake.

Third is the gift of Counsel. If we have faith and hope in God, the Holy Spirit will guide our thinking in every situation we encounter. His gentle counsel will also help us to lead others in the right direction. He's helping me as I write at this very moment; I'm confident of that. Before writing, I pray for guidance and thank Him for it in advance.

Fourth, the gift of Knowledge lets us see God's providence in everything. It makes clear to us what is right and what is wrong. It sounds so simple, but in today's world the concept of right and wrong is confusing and seems relative. It's the idea that what may be your "truth" may not be my "truth," and what's right for you may not be right for me. That's baloney!

Fifth is the gift of Fortitude. If we have strong faith, this helps us to endure all of the trials and tribulations we may face willingly for Jesus Christ. Just keep in mind always what He did for us.

Sixth is the gift of Piety. Piety keeps Christ and His Church in the forefront of our very being. This gift leads us to do God's will in all things. That must be our greatest desire.

Seven is the gift of the Fear of the Lord. This means that the last thing we want to do is offend God. If we believe in Him, love Him, and are obedient to Him, we can be assured of our salvation. If we don't "fear" God in this way, it means our faith is weak and maybe we're off track.

We all need to examine our conscience often and reassess the course of our lives periodically. It could make all the difference, so we don't want to be lackadaisical when it comes to Our Lord. Let's be frank, we all know right from wrong, for the most part. One doesn't need to be a biblical expert to know when we are doing wrong.

When we have holy thoughts and desires, that comes from the actual grace that the Holy Spirit gives us. He dwells deep within our souls, and He gives us insights constantly. The more we turn to our faith and pray, the more we will recognize the messages He sends us. When we are tuned in, it's easier to discern what is right, wrong, true, or false. We need to always stay open to the inspirations we receive from the Holy Spirit.

CHAPTER 17

Mercy

As I write this book, we have just ended what was declared the "Year of Mercy" by Pope Francis. The term "mercy" has been hijacked by some lukewarm Catholics and redefined in secular language. In their zeal to mold the Church to their own liking, they attempt to excuse sin, or lessen its impact, by saying that "God is merciful, so most people will be saved in the end." Some so-called expert theologians say we should have a reasonable hope that all people will be saved.

Well, that is a very nice thought, but it happens to be in direct contrast to the words of Christ, who referenced Hell several times. Also, very bluntly, that has never—never—been the teaching of the Holy Catholic Church.

Many Catholics believe that no matter what religion you belong to, if you are a "good person," you will go to Heaven because of God's mercy. Well, that may or may not be the case. Those who know of Christ and His life, but choose to reject Him, will not enter the eternal Kingdom of God. If they believe Jesus was just a good man, and maybe even a prophet, they will not be saved. These are the hard truths that are rejected by many Catholics who actually think all religions are equal. They believe all will be saved as a result of God's mercy.

A fellow Catholic admitted to voting for a pro-abortion candidate, and I said, "You're a Catholic, how can you do that and think it's okay?" He said, "I like the other things he stands for and, besides, God is merciful and he will forgive me." I will just say this: Any true and faithful Catholic knows that you must be truly sorry for your sins, confess them, and repent, in order to obtain forgiveness. But when one knows beforehand that something is sinful, and he or she does it anyway, that is a grave error.

Mercy is something God wants very much to offer us, but we must cooperate with Him in order to obtain it.

Being Judgmental

One of the phrases that is used very loosely to stop someone in their tracks when correcting another in matters of faith and morals is: "You're being judgmental."

The fact is that we are taught by Christ and the Church that it is our Christian duty to admonish a fellow Christian when that person is mistaken and acting against the faith. There is a term for this act, which is "fraternal correction." It is a great act of charity and mercy to point out someone's sin or mistaken belief. If you know that a friend is committing a sinful act, or is very wrong regarding a Christian truth, you may think that staying silent is the "charitable" thing to do. Saint Augustine stated that "You do worse by keeping silent than he does by sinning."

A reasonable and mature person will accept fraternal correction and, hopefully, recognize it as true mercy coming from someone who cares. If you are the person being corrected, try not to be offended. Then you can go and find the Church teaching or Bible passage yourself if you don't think the other person is justified in his or her correction. If you are the person doing the correcting, make sure you're on solid ground regarding Church teaching before you proceed to offer a correction. Again, your primary sources for these answers is the Bible and the *Catechism of the Catholic Church* (CCC).

Proverbs 10:17 says: "He who heeds instruction is on the path to life, but he who rejects reproof goes astray."

Remember, when you attempt to correct someone in the faith, do it out of true love and charity, and be gentle when you do it. I suggest that you be prepared ahead of time to prove your point if challenged. You may get some angry blowback initially, but try not to respond in kind. Believe me, I say this from experience!

As Christians, we are responsible for each other's holiness to the extent that it is possible. Surely, we can influence our family members, friends, and others we encounter in our daily lives. We should all be open to being corrected in our actions when we are doing wrong in some way. We are not perfect, right?

CHAPTER 18

Church Buildings

In this age of modernism and secularism, a school of thought has emerged that Catholic churches don't need to be "fancy," and need to be stripped down so as not to appear too ornate and ostentatious; that we need the space to be more user-friendly to the parishioners for the various activities they participate in at the church. After all, the Protestants have the right idea, which is that Jesus was simple and poor, so our churches should be stripped down and plain.

For centuries, Catholic churches were made beautiful and ornate. Back then, the biblical principles regarding the "house of God" were adhered to. The paintings and statues lifted the hearts and minds of the faithful toward Heaven. The sound of bells lovingly beckoned us to enter for the Holy Mass. The stained-glass windows reminded us of the beauty of God, Heaven, and the Church. And most important, the tabernacle containing Our Lord remained the center of it all behind or very near the altar for all to behold.

Very sadly, those days are behind us. Communion rails are gone, because no longer do we kneel down to receive the Eucharist. Modern and sometimes unrecognizable crucifixes are hanging on white-washed walls. Sometimes it's hard to even find the Stations of the Cross. And worst of all, Our Lord is placed in a back room, called a "reservation chapel," so that the congregation can speak loudly and socialize in what is now being called the "worship space."

The total misunderstanding is that it is "our church." Wrong. It is Christ's Church. It's a place we go to do one thing—and one thing only—which is to worship Him, to participate and assist in the Holy Sacrifice of the Mass. It is where Heaven and earth meet, the natural and the supernatural. It is a place where the ultimate reverence and praise should be offered by us. The time to socialize is outside or in the church hall, not in the presence of God.

Thankfully, it seems that this trend may be starting to change in some places. In some dioceses, Our Lord is being returned to the altar, and some of the new construction is exhibiting the proper style and reverence. But many dioceses are refusing to forsake their modern and mistaken ways. I've been to churches that don't resemble what a Catholic church should be in any way. We should all pray that the reverence and respect is returned to all the dioceses in the world.

Magnificent and ornate Catholic churches are a testament to the great love that we have for Jesus Christ. Why in the world we ever thought it was appropriate to house Him in a plain building that could be mistaken for a gymnasium from the outside, and then put Him in some back room out of sight, is beyond my comprehension. I hope and pray that the leaders of the Church will see the error of their ways regarding our church buildings. As respectfully as I can, I just say: What were you thinking? We do not need to build Protestant-looking churches. (Actually, I have seen some Protestant churches that look more like the Catholic churches of old.) Let's be proud of our Catholic heritage and build churches that are fitting for our eternal King, the One who created us.

CHAPTER 19

Modernism

B eginning in the nineteenth century, and continu-
ing on today, there has been a movement seeking
to change or modify the traditional teachings of the
Catholic Church. Some would say that following
Vatican II, which took place over three years, from
1962-1965, this effort kicked into high gear. We call
this unfortunate and misguided movement "modernism."

Fueling the flames of modernism was an unin-
tended consequence of the Vatican II council. Many
believe it was due to some ambiguous language contained in the council documents. Liberal bishops,
priests, and theologians began to misinterpret (some
believe purposefully and intentionally) some of the language in ways that went against established, authentic
Church teaching. This twisting of the truth became
known, wrongly, as "the spirit of Vatican II."

One of the concepts that rose to prominence after
Vatican II was that of greater "ecumenism." While it is
a commendable goal to engage more with non-Catholic churches, there was a disastrous result. Instead
of urging the Protestant Christians to come back to

Christ's original and true Catholic Church, our bishops and priests chose to make our way of doing things more like theirs.

They began teaching young Catholics that all Christian worship is basically the same. Catholicism was watered down, and emphasis was taken off of the important and necessary aspects of the Catholic Church. They could come to our churches and be welcomed, and we could go to theirs. After all, we're all Christians, right? Well, it's only right if receiving the body, blood, soul, and divinity of Our Lord in the Eucharist is not what the Church teaches it is. It's only right if the sacraments are not the channel of grace we always thought they were. It's only right if Luther and the other heretics were correct in breaking with Christ's Church. In plain words, it is not right at all.

We, as Catholic Christians, not only started acting and thinking like Protestants, we began to build our churches like theirs; we began to hear more emotion-based, feel-good, watered-down homilies. Catholics have backed away from devotions to Mary and the saints. In short, we have abandoned the faith that Christ taught us, and the Church leaders have failed the laity in the process.

While an acquaintance of mine was attending a supposed Catholic program at his Catholic church, a young woman asked the table leader this: "How do we know we'll go to Heaven?" The "trained" leader said this: "We need to say a prayer acknowledging that we sin, and then we have to accept Jesus Christ as our personal savior. That's how we will know." When I heard this, I almost hit the roof (you know, that Irish temper).

You see, that is how many, many Catholics think these days. If that doesn't bring home the fact that we need to study the true faith, I don't know what will. That answer was straight out of the Protestant playbook, and it is very wrong. Some Protestants always say, "Show me where it says that in the Bible." Well then, I ask them to show me where it sets out that way of salvation in the Bible. Not there. We all need to study our Church.

We are losing many young people to Protestantism, or they are not attending church at all, because they feel that the Church needs to change with the times and be more modern. The "old" ways of thinking and the strict rules (on abortion, contraception, euthanasia, confession, etc.) are turning them off. They feel this way because that is what many older, ignorant clergy and laity are also saying. Why stay where there are so many "rules"? They can go to a church where anything goes.

My conclusion, and that of many others, is that we have lost much of our Catholic identity. The importance of confession and the rest of the sacraments is downplayed. Young, impressionable Catholics get the idea that we are just another of the tens of thousands of denominations. They might as well go where it's easier and makes one feel good. The bishops and priests have failed miserably to pass on and teach the authentic faith. I pray for them constantly, and I hope you will, too.

In the authentic Catholic Church, there is much more to it than the feel-good fellowship and the singing of modern songs. One of the problems is that even the parents of young Catholics don't know their faith. Many of the newer priests are woefully formed in terrible seminaries that are failing miserably in teaching the faith.

I witnessed a priest give the consecrated, sacred Host to an individual who grabbed it with his finger and thumb on his right hand and said, "Thank you." The individual then carried it off. I approached the priest after Mass and said, "Didn't you realize that man wasn't Catholic?" He responded to me, "Yes, I just hope 'It' ended up in the right place." What the priest meant by the "right place" I don't have the slightest idea. But I do know that a well-formed priest who believes in the Real Presence of Christ in the Eucharist would never have offered communion to that person.

This is the type of thing we see happening in Catholic churches today. Is it any wonder why we are losing Catholics at an alarming rate? To many—even some priests—the One, Holy, Catholic, and Apostolic Church has become simply another denomination or choice among thousands.

As a result of the malformation of priests and the virtual non-formation of the laity, many have fallen prey to the fake social justice and politically correct crowd. The words "social justice" sound great; who could be against that, right? But when their actual goal goes against Church and biblical teaching, the line needs to be drawn. Several past popes and other leaders in the Church have spoken out against the evils of socialism and communism. Yet, many of the principles of these failed systems of government are being touted by many people who call themselves Catholic. Ironically, they frequently do that in the name of "social justice."

First of all, we must realize that the Church is not a political entity. We don't govern the Church based upon the mere whims of political thought. And in everything we do, including politics, we are called to adhere to the rules that Christ set down. We cannot separate our political beliefs from our Christian beliefs. When a Catholic supports and votes for a political candidate who supports abortion "rights," or supports foreigners who break our laws and enter our country illegally, or are complicit in denigrating our religious freedom, etc., that is a grave error on their part.

One cannot say, "I don't personally believe in abortion, but I support a woman's right to choose to have one," and really believe they are not also responsible for allowing that very sinful act to occur. Voting for politicians who pass these egregious laws is what allows these acts against God to occur. You can spin it and try to justify doing this all you want, but you are only kidding yourself. Wake up, Catholics!

Chapter 20

Wayward Church Leaders

Many Catholics are under the mistaken impression that we must believe everything a bishop or priest tells us. That is not true at all. The warning here is that there have always been wayward Church leaders. In fact, all of the several dangerous heresies have been promulgated by bishops and priests. Obviously, these men either never believed the true faith, or they lost it somewhere along the way. This all started with one of the original Apostles, Judas Iscariot. So always check questionable statements with the Catechism and the Bible. Knowing one's faith is the best defense against false doctrine.

At this time in the history of the world, the escalation of heresy within the Church is extremely alarming. Now, more than ever before, it behooves us to know our stuff and to not just follow blindly strange-sounding statements and programs being presented to the laity. Contrary to popular belief, the teachings of Christ and His Church cannot and will not change according to the whims and attitudes of the modern world. Do not be afraid to question a priest or bishop, or call him to task for saying or doing something contrary to the truth of the Church.

First, make sure you have reviewed the subject matter and consulted the Catechism and Bible. Always approach the priest with respect, and then make your case as clearly as you can. I've seen priests get indignant in these situations, but don't let that intimidate you. It is his job to teach the truth to the laity, and we as Christians are required to know and defend the faith.

Having said that, when you see or hear a priest or bishop who is courageous in preaching and teaching the truth, don't hesitate to compliment him and thank him. In today's world, when confusion in all things Christian abounds, these good men are fighting an uphill battle against evil and the secular forces within and surrounding the true Church. The very essence of Christianity is under vicious attacks from many quarters, and the attacks are often drenched in sweet, feel-good language that is hard to resist. Don't be fooled, be vigilant.

It is now time for the laity to speak out more and put pressure on those who are attempting to take the Church in a "new" direction based on the "modern" world. That is simply not possible; Christ and His Church will never change depending on how the wind blows at a certain time in history. Lest you think they just might succeed in their diabolical efforts, always remember that Jesus said that the gates of Hell will not prevail against the Church. We can be very confident that no matter what they do in their attempt to mold the Church into something else, they will ultimately fail. The Holy Spirit will see to that.

You noticed, I'm sure, my use of the term "dia-bolical" in the last paragraph. Believe me when I say that the Evil One is behind every effort to undermine and weaken what Christ taught us. The devil will use anyone who is open to negatively influencing the Church, and he will do it in the name of mercy, social justice, sweet language, so as to make it hard to resist. Satan will always appeal to our emotions in order to take us in and use us. The ultimate problem with that approach is that he will leave out the real truth every time.

Think about the word "truth." It seems that truth has lost its meaning in our modern world. Some say, "What's true for you may not be true for me." I have heard it said, "Well, that may be okay for him, but that's not my truth." We've all heard this kind of talk, right? But if you think about it honestly, can there be more than one truth? Absolutely not—not if you're honest with yourself.

CHAPTER 21

Is Everything Acceptable?

It's truly amazing to me that it's almost as if anything goes, as long as we don't "hurt" someone else by our actions. When a child cannot choose most things in his or her young life, but can now decide to become the opposite sex, isn't that ironic? When a sixty-year-old man who has been married and fathered children decides to "become a woman," does it shock the world? Not today. It's celebrated by many, and people say, "How brave he was to make that decision."

Never mind that God, who is perfect and cannot make a mistake, created this person as a male human being. But in today's mixed-up world, unbelievably, rather than treating individuals like this for a psychological disorder and helping them spiritually, we celebrate them and their "courage" and give them awards and see them march in parades for all to behold. Their sinful and misled actions have been legitimized, saying they are part of the LGBTQ community (lesbian, gay, bi-sexual, transgender, queer).

At this point, some politically correct-minded people may think, "Boy, the author of this book hates a lot of people." To the contrary, my friends, I actually love them. Actual and legitimate love and mercy is to let them know what Christ has taught us, what the Church has always taught, and to help others to do the same. The people with these unfortunate disorders — and that's exactly what they are — are carrying a heavy burden; it is the cross they bear. But they are not alone in their burdens.

The Bible tells us to pick up our crosses and follow Our Lord. Those who do that while being obedient in the faith will enter the Kingdom of God. It could not be any simpler to understand. Believe me, my heart breaks for the people carrying terrible burdens in their lives. The bottom line is that we are called to resist sinful behavior, and the only way to do that is to rely on God for help doing that. That is true no matter what our affliction is. I only focus on the so-called LGBTQ "community" because it is prevalent in our public discourse at this time and seems to be picking up momentum. We cannot start to legitimize wrong actions and sin in any form. To do so will surely break down the fabric of our country and the world.

As Christians, our mission is to help those who are having trouble fighting their demons and dire circumstances, whatever they may be. And we must not be afraid of the negative comments that come our way. I'm fully aware that when I voice my objections and concerns about the wrong actions occurring in society — and in the Church — some will call me uncharitable, merciless, and maybe even a religious extremist. It's really a topsy-turvy world when right becomes wrong and wrong becomes right.

It's very difficult to endure in the faith, but we can be sure that the Holy Spirit has our back and will protect us. Choosing to follow Christ's and the Church's teachings is always the choice we should make. What men say about us matters not if we are defending right from wrong. I say this knowing that we as human beings always want to appear good, fair, and proper to our fellow man. But ultimately, it's God that we must please.

Jesus warned us that there would be terrible opposition to Him, and that false teachers would always be around to confuse us and lead us astray. But he wants us to know and defend the truth at all costs. His very last statement to the Apostles was:

> Go, therefore, and make disciples of all nations, baptizing them in the name of the Father, and of the Son, and of the Holy Spirit, teaching them to observe all that I have commanded you. And behold, I am with you always, until the end of the age (Matthew 28:19-20).

CHAPTER 22

About the Catholic Bible

I t would be profitable, I believe, to discuss the Bible at this point. Over the years, I have heard many claims made about whose Bible is the legitimate one. Before I knew better, when I heard a Protestant say, "You Catholics added books to the Bible," I didn't know how to respond. When I was young, I didn't know if they were correct or not. Statements like that always made me wonder about the Catholic Church, but I didn't dig any deeper into it back then; I didn't much care. But it's amazing what one can learn if just a little effort is put into finding the truth.

The following books were left out of the Protestant version of the Bible: Tobit, Judith, Baruch, Wisdom, Sirach, 1 Maccabees, and 2 Maccabees. They also left out sections of the Book of Esther and the Book of Daniel.

The Septuagint is the oldest translation into Greek from the Hebrew Old Testament. It contains all of the books that Martin Luther left out of his version of scripture. The books contained in the Catholic Bible were settled upon back in the mid-fourth century, and this was done with the guidance of the Holy Spirit, as

Christ promised. These deleted books contained much of the early Church tradition, which Luther decided he didn't agree with. I guess he fancied himself a very powerful man.

In fact, Luther thought himself so important and righteous, he decided to consider deleting some New Testament books, such as James, which he called an "epistle of straw," and 1 Timothy and 2 Timothy. He apparently got some pushback from some of his contemporaries because the New Testament was left pretty much untouched—changing just a few words here and there.

It's obvious why Luther deleted several books for the Protestant Bible. They contain Catholic Christian teachings that he didn't believe in anymore. He was a Catholic priest, so he must have once believed in them. Things like praying for the dead and the idea of Purgatory no longer appealed to him. The Hebrew Bibles in his time didn't contain many of those passages, so Luther decided he would agree with them. It did not matter to him that he was pushing aside over 1500 years of Christian teaching and tradition. Jesus and the Apostles read and relied on the books that a mere man, a disgruntled priest, simply rejected.

I don't want to dwell on Martin Luther too long, because I and many others consider him a heretic who has done severe damage to Christians and the truths of the faith. However, I must add that he wrote and said many things that would surprise many Protestants if they knew about it. For instance, he believed polygamy was acceptable for Christians. Many of his personal statements were so offensive that you wouldn't think they came out of the mouth of a Christian. I will not go further into this subject. I only say to anyone who wants to know, the information is available. I urge you to search for it. You might look at the real Martin Luther in a new light.

In addition to Luther, some of the other "reformers" were Andreas Karlstadt, Philip Melanchthon, Huldrych Zwingli, and John Calvin. All of these men broke away from the real Christian Church and went astray. You can look them up, if you care to. Suffice it to say that what they all did was very dangerous and an extremely grave lapse in judgment. We as human beings cannot add or subtract that which came directly from God, much as some may try. Only God knows for sure whether or not they repented before their deaths. I hope they did. The problem is that their heresy lives on in the lives of unsuspecting and unknowing Protestants who love God very much.

CHAPTER 23

The Essence of Prayer

Prayer is very important in the lives of Christians. It consists of many things, including giving thanks to God, appealing to Him for help, praying for others, praying for situations, and prayers of adoration and worship.

All forms of prayer are good if offered in faith and for right and moral reasons. God listens to all prayers when offered from the heart. He answers all prayers in one way or the other. Shallow prays, self-centered prayers, and prayers for more "stuff" may go unanswered. But then again, that probably IS your answer.

Prayers don't have to go on and on and on with flowery, sweet-sounding words. Sometimes a very simple prayer will suffice. You can pray a one-word prayer by saying "Jesus" and focusing on His being with you. You can look at something beautiful and say, "Thank you." God will know what you mean.

Many of the prayers said by Catholics have come down through the ages from the saints and Fathers of the Church. Their beautiful prayers and meditations help us in the things we ought to say sometimes, but don't always have the words for. We internalize what is being prayed in these age-old prayers and make them our own. But a belief in what these prayers are saying is necessary for them to be fruitful and efficacious.

We have many beautiful prayers that come straight out of the language of scripture. Jesus himself taught the Apostles what we call the Our Father. The Apostles' Creed and the Nicene Creed are prayers of affirmation and belief in what Christ passed on to us. The words of the Hail Mary come directly out of the Bible, in which we ask Our Blessed Mother to pray for us, to intercede with her Son on our behalf.

I've heard from many Protestants, and many Catholics who are heavily influenced by Protestants, who say that Catholic prayers are "rote," or too repetitious; that we say the words but don't really pay attention to what they mean. They believe the only way to pray is to pray off the top of one's head, in one's own words, and that it will mean much more. Well, there's nothing wrong with doing just that. But I know from experience that the prayers Protestants say — for instance, before meals — are also "rote." Yet, they don't see it that way. Do they honestly think they say something different every time. They don't. But that's okay. Most times, before a meal, I like to say grace with a short Catholic prayer, which is, "Bless us, O Lord, and these Thy gifts, which we are about to receive from Thy bounty, through Christ Our Lord. Amen." That says it all. In special or certain circumstances, I may add something to this prayer. There's no wrong way to pray.

I myself say several old, traditional Catholic prayers at night when I retire, but I also add personal prayers for family members, friends, our country and the world, the poor, the sick and suffering, etc. I repeat, all prayer is good. It's not fruitful or necessary to criticize how another prays. We just need to do it a lot. Say amen. Amen!

One can obtain Catholic prayer books, which contain wonderful old, traditional prayers, how to pray the rosary, how to pray the Divine Mercy Chaplet, meditations, novenas, etc. There are apps you can get on your cell phone that include the complete Bible, prayers, the Catechism, information on confession, Vatican documents, and a whole range of Catholic content. Most of this content is free. Check it out.

One of my personal favorite things is to pray the Stations of the Cross, also called the Way of the Cross. This prayer takes us briefly, but powerfully, through the passion, death, and resurrection of Jesus Christ. It's a stark and beautiful reminder of how much Our Lord loves us and what He did for us. It never hurts to be reminded of what it's all about. If you've never prayed the Way of the Cross, or haven't done it for a while, I urge you to do so. Praying the mysteries of the rosary is also a beautiful way to meditate on the life of Jesus Christ.

With the knowledge and belief that God loves us and desires that we join Him in Heaven when our time is up in this world, we must realize that to worship and adore Him is of utmost importance. He wants us to think of Him in all we do and expects us to do so. Prayer is a most important activity for human beings to engage in. Just like having faith, praying is an act of the will. When we pray, we are telling God: "Lord, I believe in you, and I know you will answer me in a way that bests serves You, and I know You will provide what I need."

One could say that prayers of adoration, worship, and gratitude are the highest form of pray. Spending time in front of the Blessed Sacrament in complete silence, contemplating the fact that He is really present in the consecrated, glorified Host within the tabernacle, or exposed in a monstrance, is a truly awesome and blessed experience. I highly recommend doing that as much as possible.

The Mass itself, the Our Father, the Hail Mary, the Angelus, and others, are examples of what are called vocal prayers that are said both in public and private. Prayers of meditation—again, such as the rosary—lead us to a deeper understanding of the mysteries of the faith. Some things we will never understand while in this world. I'll just add that reading scripture and doing other spiritual reading also falls into the category of meditation.

Contemplative prayer consists of focusing on God and His love and greatness, which can be wordless prayer. In silence, one can listen for any inspiration He may send our way. Believe me, when you are truly tuned in, it can happen. During contemplative prayer, always keep in mind what Jesus Christ did for us. I mention this because there is a practice many Catholics have been exposed to, which is called "centering prayer." It calls for a complete emptying of one's mind and the use of a mantra. This is nothing more than a repackaging of the Hindu practice of transcendental meditation for unsuspecting Catholics. It was promoted by some wayward and misled priests in the 1970s as part of the New Age movement that has been active in the Catholic Church for decades. One can find plenty of books and articles warning Catholics to stay far away from this dangerous practice.

Saint Paul, in 1 Thessalonians 5:18, tells us to "give thanks in all circumstances." It should go without saying—but I'll say it anyway—that we should always give thanks to Our Lord. We have much to be thankful for, especially the completely unselfish sacrifice Christ made for our benefit.

Many of us turn to God when we think we "need" something, or when we're in trouble, but we tend to forget about Him when all is well. I'm sure you will agree that that is very shallow indeed. However, it is true that God wants us to turn to Him in times of need. But it is important to note that when we appeal to Our Lord, our wants and desires must be just and rightly ordered. We will not always get what we pray for, but we will always get what we need. Keep in mind, though, what we need might be spiritual and not temporal. That is ultimately what is most important and in our best interest.

Looking back on my life, there were many times when my prayers seemed to go unanswered. Sometimes they were answered in a way I hadn't expected, although I didn't realize it at the time. It's best just to trust in complete faith that Our Father has our most important interests in mind. I find it comforting at this stage of my life to just pray, "Your will be done in all things, Lord."

It is also very important that we ask God's forgiveness for our sins. It is okay to talk to God yourself, but Christ gave us sacramental confession through His priests, and this is necessary to receive the absolution and grace we all need for salvation. Sadly, many Catholics have been influenced by outside forces and no longer believe they need to confess to a priest. To them I say: Please consider returning to confession. Remember that it is a sacrament through which we receive much grace, and it helps one to avoid sin. I will refer you to two examples from scripture regarding confession, but there are others: Matthew 9:2-8 and John 20:23. Believe me, this is not a sacrament we can avoid; it's a tremendous gift, so accept it!

Partly due to our busy and cluttered lives, many of us just forget to pray. One way to resolve this problem is to form a habit of praying at certain times — at night before turning in, in the morning before rising, and before meals. Think about making prayer a priority in your daily routine. It would please Our Lord tremendously.

CHAPTER 24

How Many Are Saved?

I briefly touched on this subject earlier, but I will now go into the subject of salvation a little more deeply.

As I stated before, it has become popular and almost common these days to believe that Hell probably doesn't really exist. The topic of Hell rarely comes up in homilies and is not emphasized in classes on the faith. The Catholic bishops, priests, and catechists have failed the laity miserably for many decades when it comes to this all-important subject. After all, when one boils it all down, it's all about going either to Heaven or Hell. What we do in this worldly life is for all the marbles. All instruction by bishops, priests, and catechists should focus on saving souls, helping us get to Heaven.

There is an unfortunate body of thought out there that if one is just a "good person," and doesn't hurt anyone, and observes most of the Ten Commandments, it will be enough to merit Heaven when we die. Well, that couldn't be further from the truth, according to Christ and His Church.

Matthew 7:21-23 teaches us this important point, as follows:

[21]Not everyone who says to me, "Lord, Lord," will enter the kingdom of heaven, but only the one who does the will of my Father in heaven. [22]Many will say to me on that day, "Lord, Lord, did we not prophesy in your name? Did we not drive out demons in your name? Did we not do mighty deeds in your name?" [23]Then I will declare to them solemnly, "I never knew you. Depart from me, you evildoers."

For your further edification, read these verses in scripture: Philippians 2:12; 1 Corinthians 10:11-12; 2 Timothy 2:11-13; Hebrews 10:26-27.

There are many more, but you get the point. We must constantly work on our own salvation, hopefully with the help of our leaders in the Church.

On the specific subject of Hell, Our Lord made it crystal clear that if we don't do what's necessary, we can surely go there. It's hard to comprehend that many people, including bishops and priests, have come to the conclusion that Christ didn't really mean it when He made emphatic statements about the possibility of going to Hell. Are we able to re-create Christ and make Him something other than what He said He was, and can we reinterpret his plain words to our own liking, thereby lessening the effects of sin? I'm pretty sure we cannot do that. I wouldn't want to base my salvation on that selfish and politically correct version of scripture.

When one says, "God is merciful," that doesn't mean that He will accept anything we do and just let us into Heaven anyway. True mercy is knowing and teaching the truth of the Christian faith. Yes, some truths are hard to accept, and avoiding sin is extremely difficult. But we are to pick up our cross and carry it, whatever our personal burdens may be. In Christ's mercy, He offers us forgiveness and grace if we humbly and truly seek it. Sacramental confession is our vehicle to seek it.

Please review these verses regarding the existence of Hell: Matthew 25:41; Matthew 25:46; Luke 3:16-17; 2 Thessalonians 1:6-9.

There are several sections of scripture in both the Old and New Testaments referring to Hell. Please do not accept the false teaching that God is so merciful that no matter what you do will be forgiven and you will be accepted into Heaven regardless of your sins. Christ and His Church have never, ever taught that, and no one can change that fact.

To strengthen what I have just laid out for you, here are some quotes by some saints and Doctors of the Church:

> Saint Augustine: "Not all, nor even a majority, are saved."

> Saint Alphonsus Liguori: "The greater part of men choose to be damned rather than to love Almighty God."

> Saint John of the Cross: "Behold how many there are who are called, and how few who are chosen! And behold, if you have no care for yourself, your perdition is more certain than your amendment, especially since the way that leads to eternal life is so narrow."

Saint Vincent Ferrer: "Many religious go straight to Hell because they do not keep their vows."

Saint John Neumann: "Notwithstanding assurances that God did not create any man for Hell, and that He wishes all men to be saved, it remains equally true that only few will be saved; that only few will go to Heaven; and that the greater part of mankind will be lost forever."

Saint Anselm: "If you would be quite sure of your salvation, strive to be among the fewest of the few. Do not follow the majority of mankind, but follow those who renounce the world and never relax their efforts day or night so that they may attain everlasting blessedness."

Boiling it all down, it's abundantly clear that to achieve salvation and eternity in Heaven, we must really work at it and desire it. We cannot just pick and choose from the "rules" God laid out for us. We must accept them all and do our very best to adhere to them. Going to church is all-important, and participating in all of the sacraments will give us the grace God wants us so desperately to have. We have been given sacramental confession to return us to a state of grace when we fall — and there is no doubt that we all fall sometimes.

CHAPTER 25

The Four Last Things

We as Christians believe that the four last things of man, which will occur when we die and our souls leave this world, are Death, Judgment, Heaven, or Hell. If one doesn't believe this, then he or she is not a Christian. All Christians, Catholic and non-Catholic, agree on this important teaching.

At Mass, we profess that Jesus Christ will come again to judge the living and the dead. There are many passages in the Bible referring to the end of this world. Christ himself mentioned His Second Coming often, and He referred to the many signs that would lead up to and signal this upcoming event. There will be a tremendous loss of faith, and false prophets will appear on the scene. There will be many natural disasters, such as earthquakes, hurricanes, tornadoes, tidal waves, etc. There will be famine and sickness, and wars will exist on a great scale. Sound familiar?

Of course, we know that we will all die some day and in some way; so it's just a matter of when and how, right? None of us like to think much about death. In fact, we do as much as we can to avoid it—but there's no cure for death in this world. The good news is that we can plan for eternity in the next world. Can we do what it takes to receive a good outcome in the end, or are we just too busy enjoying ourselves and getting all we can while we're in the here and now?

The Catechism says this: "God's triumph over the revolt of evil will take the form of the Last Judgment after the cosmic upheaval of this passing world" (CCC 677).

Jesus said, "Those who have done right shall rise to life; the evildoers shall rise to be damned" (John 5:29).

What is being described in the last two quotes is called the General Judgment, when the battle between good and evil has come to an end.

Now, backing up a bit, the Church teaches that when one dies prior to the end of the world, he or she faces what is called the Particular Judgment immediately. There will be no delay in knowing where we will spend all of eternity.

The vast majority of us—those who are actually going to Heaven—will spend time in Purgatory before we can behold the face of God, also called the beatific vision. No one can behold the presence of God without being purified "as through fire." Unlike the fires of Hell, Purgatory affords us a cleansing, purifying, holy fire that will rid us of the many temporal, venial sins we carried with us at the time of death. We are able to lessen our time in Purgatory by making sure we worry more about God's will than our own in this life.

CHAPTER 26

Scandal in the Church

Throughout the history of the Church, there have been many, many heresies, and false teachers have always been present, especially within the Church. When I say that, yes, I am talking about wayward cardinals, bishops, priests, and nuns—and even an occasional pope. Some of these individuals were not well-formed in the Catholic faith, and some have had evil intent. Many simply lost their faith, and many never really believed it in the first place.

There exists strong evidence that there has been an actual infiltration of the Church by individuals whose intent it was to disrupt and damage the Church. Also, over the last fifty or sixty years, the Catholic Church has become a "safe" haven for homosexuals to hide and practice their sinful acts. In fact, many have risen in stature to become bishops, who then promoted their "own kind" to also become bishops. Priests of their "own kind" have been and are treated better than obedient and faithful priests. Many priests are now speaking out about the sexual and mental abuse they experienced while in seminary or while trying to be a good priest. And more and more men are revealing that they were sexually abused by priests while being an altar boy or seminarian. This grave problem is now being exposed like never before in the Church's history. It is entirely possible that Our Lord has decided to purge these evil prelates and priests from His Church. The laity needs to step up strongly against these sinful bishops and priests. When so many in the hierarchy of the Church are corrupt, who else does the responsibility fall on but true believers within the Church? It's us, brothers and sisters.

The result of this evil infiltration has also been a severe watering down of the actual Catholic faith. The worst result of this great problem is a loss of reverence for the Blessed Sacrament. Tabernacles containing Our Lord have been removed from altars all over the world and relegated to backrooms that are now called "reservation chapels." Church naves are now used for all sorts of events, like musical concerts. It's now more important that choirs be placed in front by the altars so as to entertain us, while the singers sway and clap at times. Talking loudly in church before the Mass begins is widely accepted as a "joyful noise," and I've heard it said that Jesus loves this. I disagree, as do many others.

Never mind readying our hearts and minds to receive the Eucharist, praying, and reverently contemplating the Sacrifice of the Mass. It's all about us now. To that, I say we have seriously lost our way, and weak bishops and priests have led us "off the cliff" in this regard. I pray that the Holy Catholic Church, with the intercession of Our Lady and the mercy of her Son, can be returned to what it once was. We belong to the

Church Jesus Christ founded. As Catholics, we should never forget that fact no matter how bad things get.

The recent scandals plaguing the Church are directly related to bad leadership. A purging has begun, thank God. I urge all Catholics to hold your priests to account when you see or hear something contrary to Church teaching. In order to do that, we must know our faith; we can't just "shoot from the hip," so to speak. If a priest or deacon gives a questionable homily, and you know it, speak up in a charitable way. It's also our responsibility to pass on the faith to others. It's hard to do that when we don't know it ourselves.

The best and most efficacious way to help strengthen the Church is to pray, pray, and pray more. Our Lord will hear you, believe me. The mother of Jesus will also intercede and pray for the Church; just ask her. One of the most potent weapons we have against evil in this world is the rosary. Please don't underestimate its power. The Way of the Cross, also called the Stations of the Cross, is another very important way to meditate on what Christ did for us.

The time of silence on the part of good prelates, priests, and the laity is now over. The spiritual war is well underway, I would say, in a bigger way than ever before in history. Get involved and jump into the breach. Jesus himself wants and needs our effort to repair His Holy Catholic Church. Don't sit on the sidelines anymore if you care about the state of the faith around the world.

CHAPTER 27

To Protestants and Lapsed Catholics

If you've read this book up to this point, I will make this plea to all of you. We are in a time of great turmoil in this world. There is much hate and war going on in every quarter. In my lifetime, I've never seen it so bad. In fact, it's accelerating at a disturbing pace.

Because of a backing away from the spiritual, a loss of faith in the Almighty, and a strengthening focus on the things of this world, we as the people of God are in deep trouble. A great perversion of marriage, the family, and many other sacred things, is taking place in our overwhelmingly secular world. The truth of the Gospel and the right way of life has been pushed aside, and we can't talk about that for fear of not being "politically correct." For all intents and purposes, good has become bad, and bad has become good.

Abortion, for instance, is unbelievably called "women's health care" instead of the murder that it is of an actual person. We are told to believe that it is a woman's choice to either accept or reject the life growing within her. I don't believe God looks at it that way. But I guess one needs to believe in God to accept that statement. The individuals who say they do believe, and yet they are "pro-choice," are merely kidding themselves.

Another area that has deteriorated in the Christian sphere is the outlook on contraception. In case you are unaware, all—I repeat, all—Christian churches opposed artificial contraception until August of 1930, when the Anglican church found it acceptable during their Lambeth Conference of bishops. Those bishops decided, basically, that if a woman decided she had a "moral obligation to limit or avoid parenthood," and it was decided on "Christian principles," contraception was acceptable. After that, other Protestant denominations fell into line. Not surprisingly, abortion was easier to accept after that, and many Christian denominations now support it.

The Catholic Church is the only one that has remained steadfast in its teaching that contraception and abortion are not acceptable in any way, shape, or form. As a result, they say we as Catholics are living "in the dark ages," and so forth. To that, I say that the Church of Jesus Christ doesn't bend to the whims and sinful desires of this world. In fact, it should be just the opposite!

I want to now address my comments to Catholics who have left the Church for some reason. Whether your exit was due to the various sexual abuse scandals, or maybe you felt you weren't being "fed" by a boring priest, or you just didn't want to follow the strict "rules" of the Church, I want you to know that we would welcome you back with open arms. It's probably not your fault that you didn't really know the faith. As I've already said, over the last half century, the teachers of the faith have fallen down on the job in a major way. It's hard to understand or pass on the teachings of the Church when you were never taught them.

I promise that if you make it a priority to learn the history of the Church, study the Catechism, which is totally based on biblical teachings and the oral Tradition of the Church, you will want to come running back.

To all non-Catholic Christians I want you to know that we consider you our brothers and sisters in Christ. But to the point, respectfully, you are not getting the fullness of the faith that Christ passed on to us. I don't say this in a condescending way, but out of love and concern. I realize that most of you have grown up Protestant, and that's what you are familiar with. I also know that many of you have been taught many myths and have been fed a lot of misinformation about what Catholics believe.

There have been many, many people who have made the journey to the Catholic Church, and they were once in your shoes. The reason is because they took it upon themselves to seek the truth. After doing their necessary due diligence and study, they made the only decision that made sense.

Now, you might say that those who converted were probably misled or convinced out of ignorance to do so. Well, to that I say this: Many, many of these converts were Protestant ministers from various denominations. Wouldn't you agree that they probably knew the Bible very well? I know your answer to that question. Why would a non-Catholic Christian pastor, who earned his or her living doing that, decide he or she wanted to be a Catholic?

I asked that exact question to a gentleman speaking at a Catholic church about his conversion. Following his very compelling and animated talk, he took questions from those in attendance. I raised my hand and he picked me. I asked him this exact question: "If you had to pick one main reason you converted to Catholicism, what would it be?" His answer to me consisted of one word: TRUTH. He needed to say no more.

I can't remember that fellow's name, but there are several prominent Protestant converts that I could name, and they have written books and given talks all over the world. Some of them are:

Marcus Grodi, a former Presbyterian minister, who founded the Coming Home Network and hosts *The Journey Home* television program on EWTN;

Scott Hahn, professor at Franciscan University and teacher/speaker extraordinaire on the Catholic Church;

Stephen Ray, a learned former evangelical Baptist and teacher of biblical studies;

Paul Thigpen, Ph.D., a former evangelical Protestant;

Dr. Allen Hunt, former pastor of a megachurch with over 15,000 congregants each week;

David Currie, who received a degree from Trinity International University, and whose father was a fundamentalist preacher;

Devin Rose, a former evangelical Protestant and now a Catholic apologist and writer about the faith;

Thomas Howard, a renowned professor and former evangelical Protestant; and

Dr. Taylor Marshall, a former Anglican priest, now a Catholic philosopher, author, and professor.

This is only a short list of the scores of smart, informed, and studied people who have converted to Catholicism. Believe me, they didn't do so out of ignorance. I think you can see that based on their credentials. By the way, all of these gentlemen were so convinced of their decision to become Catholic that they wrote books about it. Some have written several books and have developed CDs and Bible studies on the faith. Check them out. I have them all in my personal library, which continues to grow.

Now, it's true that the men I just listed are very smart and educated people, but many thousands of converts are average people who happen to love Our Lord and wanted to make sure they had it right regarding the Church and their salvation.

I have read and heard stories of hundreds of converts to the Catholic Church. They come from many, many denominations. Even though all of the stories are different, it seems that there is a common thread running through them: TRUTH.

Chapter 28

A Conversion Story

The following is the conversion story of an individual named Tim, who went in search of the truth after starting to question what he believed all his life. You might find that you have some things in common with this fine man.

"My name is Tim. I grew up in a Protestant home. My first recollection of church was in a southern Baptist church in El Toro, California. I remember going to Sunday school and sitting in church with my family every Sunday. Lessons learned and sermons that I heard on Sundays were reaffirmed in my home during the week. My family would always pray and read from the Bible. At a very young age, God became a very important part of my life. I really learned to love God and wanted to know more about Him by reading the Bible.

"I am reminded of a song that I used to sing as a young boy: 'Read your Bible, pray every day, pray every day, pray every day; read your Bible, pray every day, and you'll grow, grow, grow….' This concept was taught to me as I grew in the faith — that we get closer to God by reading the Bible and having a closer relationship with Him through prayer.

"On June 10, 1981, I was six years old when I asked my mom how to ask Jesus to come into my heart. I had heard many young people and adults in the congregation talk about being saved and how Jesus came into their hearts as their Lord and Savior. Even then, I wanted Jesus to be part of my life, and I didn't want to miss out on Heaven. I asked Mom how I could be saved. She prayed a simple prayer with me, asking Jesus to come into my heart. Shortly thereafter, we met with our pastor of El Toro Baptist Church, and he underlined a verse in my Bible that I still remember today. It was Romans 10:9, which says, 'for if you confess with your mouth that Jesus is Lord and believe in your heart that God raised Him from the dead, you will be saved.'

"As I continued to grow up in the church, these concepts were further strengthened while attending more Sunday school, Bible studies, youth groups, etc. We moved quite a bit due to my dad being in the military. I remember looking for different churches with my parents as we moved around the country. When other kids asked me what religion I was, I said I was a Baptist. That was until we attended a Protestant chapel in Monterey, California, while my dad was attending Naval Postgraduate School there. It was my first exposure to other Protestant denominations. The basic outline of the church that I was used to was there, but there was a different emphasis on tradition, and the biblical interpretations weren't quite the same in some instances. I even participated in the services as an acolyte. That was not something I had seen before in the Baptist church. I began to realize that other Christian denominations worshipped in similar ways but may emphasize certain parts of worship differently. I remember having conversations with my parents about which Protestant church was correct, and I asked them what we believed. The answer was always, 'The Bible.'

"We then moved to Virginia and found a 'non-denominational' church in Springfield called Immanuel Bible Church. It made a lot of sense to me that if it was all about God's Word, we should be going to a Bible church to study His Word. I attended more Sunday school, Sunday evening youth group, Bible studies, and youth choir practice. I continued to grow in my faith and my personal relationship with Jesus Christ.

"I remember having some friends that were Catholic during this time in my life. I had been taught that Catholics believed that a person had to earn their way to Heaven, that they did not see salvation as a free gift. From my understanding of the history of the Protestant Reformation, the Catholic Church was corrupted at some point, and the Protestant Reformation had returned the Church to the way God had intended. It did not dawn on me until later in my life to consider why there were so many Protestant sects. Why did they have different beliefs? Why was the Catholic Church the same everywhere?

"While finishing up high school and entering college, I drifted away from my Bible reading and prayer, and I missed church frequently. My attendance was sporadic, unfortunately. It seemed that my priorities were more in line when I was younger. This brings to mind the rest of the song I referred to earlier, which I sung as a young boy: '…Don't read your Bible, forget to pray, forget to pray, forget to pray; don't read your Bible, forget to pray, and you'll shrink, shrink, shrink.'

"While I was in college, I struggled to find a church that was similar to the Bible church that I grew up in. I kept trying different denominations. Jesus was still very important to me even as I was struggling. I was still of the belief that Christianity was all only about the Bible. I would later come to discover that the term for believing in the Bible alone is *sola scriptura*.

"Toward the end of my college days, I met and fell in love with my beautiful wife, Heather. God was very important to both of us. She was a Catholic, and I was—well, when others asked about my religion, I would respond, 'I'm Christian.' I didn't want to say 'Protestant' because there are so many denominations in existence. I remained headstrong and stuck to my belief in *sola scriptura*. But I can say that the Lord Heather believed in, as a Catholic, was the same Lord I had come to know and love.

"I attended my first Catholic Mass with Heather and her family. I remember just being lost. She told me to basically follow everything she did. During the Mass, the priest said to offer one another a sign of peace. Heather turned to me, leaned in and said, 'Peace be with you,' while kissing me on the cheek. Well, the woman next to me, whom I didn't know, received quite a surprise when I turned to her and said, 'Peace be with you,' giving her a little peck on the cheek.

"Heather and I were married in the Catholic Church because I knew that was extremely important to her and her family. I never imagined getting married in a Catholic Church, and I was not extremely happy about it. I thought that this would just be for the wedding, and the rest of our lives we would find a 'compromise'; that we would look for one of the many Protestant denominations out there that would have traditions somewhat like the Catholic Church, but would focus on the Bible alone, or *sola scriptura*.

"We moved around the country, due to my own military career this time, and tried many different churches. We settled on a Lutheran church in one state, a Presbyterian in another state, and a Baptist church in yet another state. However, Heather was always being called back to the Catholic Church. When I was on deployment, she would always attend a Catholic Church. At one point, Heather asked me to try the Catholic Church, but I was really digging my heels in, based on my ignorance and misconceived notions of Catholicism. I bought into the myths I had heard over the years.

"I was confident that I knew the truth based on what I had learned all those years as a Protestant. I believed strongly that Jesus was and is my Savior, but I also believed that my faith was based on the Bible alone. And I wrongly believed that Catholics prayed to Mary as if she too were God. The next several years turned out to be eye-opening ones.

"Honestly, I did not do much research on my own until my father-in-law began to gently question me during our many conversations about the differences between Protestantism and Catholicism. He asked me a question that really went to the heart of the matter. He said, 'If Protestantism is the true Church of Christ, then why are there tens of thousands of Protestant

denominations, which hold so many different interpretations of scripture? How does that line up with *sola
scriptura*? And if the Bible alone is your guide, where is
that concept in the Bible?'

"I started to read and study on my own, and my
father-in-law and I continued our conversations, during
which I peppered him with questions. After attending
a Mass with Heather's family, I made a comment that I
really didn't get that much out of the homily given by
the priest. I was used to highly upbeat messages in our
Protestant sermons. I wasn't really 'fed' by that priest.
Heather's father said, 'The Mass is not only about the
homily. In fact, it's probably the least important part.
We Catholics attend Mass to be "fed" the actual body
and blood of Jesus Christ and to participate in the
re-presentation of the sacrifice of Christ.'

"Not totally understanding this, I thought, could
it really be possible to receive the actual body and blood
of Our Lord? What a miracle it would be if this were
true! I wanted to know more, and I thought it couldn't
hurt anything or anybody if I studied and took classes
to learn the Catholic perspective.

"I began attending RCIA classes and quickly real-
ized how ignorant I was about the Catholic Church
and its teachings. I began to understand and believe
that the Catholic Church is the one true Church — the
Church that Christ started with Peter, as the first earthly
leader after Jesus ascended. I have come to believe that
the Protestant Reformation caused some in the Church
to break with Jesus' Church and go in a different direction. When Christ said the Holy Spirit will be with the

Church until the end of time, why would Luther and company do that?

"As a Protestant, I failed to understand where the authority for interpreting scripture came from. Was it each pastor? And which denomination had it right? It was a huge revelation to me when I learned that the Church teachings were passed on through Apostolic succession. This means that bishops and priests, who are ordained in a direct line from the Apostles, can then consecrate the bread and wine for our consumption, and then pass on the teachings of the faith.

"In the Presbyterian church, we would recite the Apostles' Creed. I always wondered why we stated, 'I believe in the Holy Spirit, the Holy Catholic Church....' I always thought we were referring to the early Church that Christ established with the Apostles. Jesus said in Matthew 16:18. 'And I say to you that you are Peter, and upon this rock I will build my Church, and the gates of Hell shall not prevail against it.' Why would Jesus allow His true Church to become corrupt and then splinter off thousands of times? I now realize that the Catholic Church is the One, Holy, Catholic, and Apostolic Church, and it was gently calling me home.

"I have now been a Catholic for three years, and I love participating in the Mass and receiving Our Lord's body, blood, soul and divinity. Attending Church now has so much more meaning in my life. I used to speak of having a 'personal relationship' with Jesus. Now I know that receiving the Eucharist affords me the most personal relationship with Him that I could ever have otherwise.

"I'm still learning and studying Catholicism, and I know that I am home in the right and true Church. I am eternally grateful to those who have helped me 'come home.' In that, I include my wife, Heather, and my father-in-law. They gave me space and time when I needed to consider and pray about what I was hearing.

"Heather and I, and our three children—Sean, Brooke, and Leigh—are currently members of St. Aloysius Catholic parish in Leonardtown, Maryland, where we continue to learn more about God's graces, blessings, and designs for our lives. We look forward to helping our children grow in the Catholic faith as we all get closer to Christ through His sacraments."

I will now reveal to you that Tim is my son-in-law, and his wife, Heather, is my oldest child. As long as I've known Tim, he has been a faithful Christian. He comes from a wonderful Christian family. I very much enjoyed the many respectful conversations we have had—and continue to have—over the years. I must admit that we did enjoy a few cigars and a wee bit of Irish whiskey once in a while during our talks.

CHAPTER 29

A Plea to All Christians

We are living in perilous times. Christianity is being threatened as never before in the history of man. There have been more martyrs for the faith in the twentieth century than in all other centuries combined.

It is now time to unify as Christians. The only way to do that is to return to the Church that Christ actually started, the Catholic Church. We want you back. Don't be afraid or apprehensive. We will help you learn what you need to know. Right now, you are not receiving all the grace you could be getting from the sacraments of the Church, which Christ gave us to sustain us in this world.

We Catholics aren't telling you that you are wrong in what you're doing, in most cases. We're not questioning your love for God. It's just that you're not receiving all that God meant for you to receive. Will you get to Heaven if you stay in your present situation? Only God knows the answer to that. Our Church teaches that you may, but maybe it will be more difficult. Should we do all that we can do to achieve our place in Heaven? Absolutely!

Just imagine what a worldwide reunification of all Christians would mean for the salvation of the world. It would be a major blessing to humanity. I believe that Jesus Christ would be overjoyed. If we could just be unified in all of the perennial Catholic Church teachings, it would be a force against evil to behold on behalf of Our Lord.

Don't let the failures of many of the Church leaders affect how you perceive the Catholic Church. They don't represent Christ when they ignore the truth and commit crimes and sins within the Church. They will get their just reward one day. The majority of bishops and priests belong totally to Jesus Christ and are true to His teachings and His Church.

We must look to the future of Christianity in the present world, while concentrating on the next world, which will last for eternity. Remember, Christ taught us that the path to destruction (Hell) is wide, and the path to Heaven is narrow. The next move is yours.

God bless you all.

About the Author

Paul A. Nelson converted to the Catholic Church at age sixteen. His journey included leaving the Church temporarily but returning after a startling, life-changing experience.

Nelson studied Christianity for years and today is a Consecrated Marian Catechist, having studied the extensive catechetical coursework of the late Servant of God Father John Hardon.

Nelson's main focus is his own faith in God, his family, and his strong desire to put forth the truth of Christ. He and his wife, Nancy, reside in Williamsburg, Virginia.

About Leonine Publishers

Leonine Publishers LLC makes fine Catholic literature available to Catholics throughout the English-speaking world. Leonine Publishers offers an innovative "hybrid" approach to book publication that helps authors as well as readers. Please visit our web site to learn more about us. Browse our online bookstore to find more solid Catholic titles to uplift, challenge, and inspire.

Our patron and namesake is Pope Leo XIII, a prudent, yet uncompromising pope during the stormy years at the close of the 19th century. Please join us as we ask his intercession for our family of readers and authors.

www.leoninepublishers.com